Duration, Endurance, Adventure, Herbs Trees and Commodity Energy Conservation Education

By: Richard Wright

First Edition

ISBN # 9798218765163

Table of Contents

Introduction

Fishing on a lake to prepare for the Fourth of July Festivities to show up with a freshwater fish instead of empty handed is a good lesson to start. Some of my favorite memories include myself, my siblings, and my parents. Each of us caught fish on charter boat ventures to include red snapper and most of us caught grouper, some of the trolling brought in Spanish mackerel, I think that's a king mackerel. There were trophies at the neighborhood lake fishing, the picture and fond memories associated with the outing not to not mention the food energy from fish in the ocean are something I hope to continue planning for and the biggest challenge is how to improve resilience to sustain those journeys to catch fish when forecasting out 1,000 years many of the means of travel transportation will have to revert to pre-industrial age. My educating myself on this fact have caused me to not plan some travels such as snow skiing on mogul-laden slopes that I think I need, or missed, and I should have ensured to plan a better substitute for the longer distance traveling, so that 'getaways' to socialize among my siblings and parents continues. So, I have to think about good more near distance ways to bring the family to have fun on retreats of the sort. When not educating ourselves, we work and have fun adventures. Parents to me earned college degrees, each of my siblings and myself have college degrees, I earned a Masters degree and so did my twin sister, my oldest brother earned a Masters degree, and my younger sibling got certified as a nurse. Some of my favorite memories include holidays, Thanksgiving among cousins and aforementioned, Christmas Eve and Christmas day gatherings, and summer vacation travels.

A Lesson From Selling Books, Data, and Adventuring

Before I begin storytelling and information sharing, let me discuss with you how to save some money with reducing and rationing your electricity. One of the first things I learned in sales school training at Southwestern Co. selling books, was to take cold showers. I spent most of the summer morning showers during my junior to senior year break between college classes taking really fast showers because the water was so cold I didn't want to be in the shower for long. This had a benefit of first, reducing water heating that is normally a want during that season, and reduction of non-need water consumption. Depending on the length of time someone is in the shower, they use a varying amount of electricity. While "old showers" use "five gallons of water a minute," according to https://water.usgs.gov/edu/activity-percapita.php. Dishwashers use six to 16 gallons of water, with newer EnergyStar models using six gallons, accordingly. Whereas washing machines are the worst user of heated water at 25 to 40 gallons per load, so it may be advisable to use cold water with your clothes.

I have recently elaborated my wonder about that by researching sinkholes to small amount, and that would depend more on the underlying geologic structure of where water, other liquids, and semi-solid liquids, are found. To prevent sinkholes, I presume, I read in "Twilight in The Desert" that sand is put back into where petroleum reserves are fully vacant. Although, I am not a geologist, there is rock structure that I know fracking must go through so that's why industrial diamonds and platinum are utilized in drilling for natural resources such as gasoline, based on my reading of the World Book Encyclopedia excerpt on components of unrefined oil. Now, I recently bought a "Rocks & Minerals of North America" book by National Geographic that describes sinkholes having a likelihood to "occur in regions underlain by bedrock that is easily dissolved in groundwater. Examples are carbonate rocks and evaporite deposits such as salt and gypsum." (155 National Geographic) Although, "Massive gypsum beds are known as alabaster. Gypsum is mined to produce cement, Sheetrock, and fertilizer." (43 Nat'l. Geo.) "The movement of groundwater causes the rock to dissolve over time...leaves the bedrock unable to support the surface, and the land collapses into the hole." (155 Nat'l Geo.) "Anhydrite is harder and has three good cleavage planes that create cubic-like fragments." (43 Nat'l. Geo.). Salt is a solid, chlorine is a gas under certain circumstances such as waves crashing into a semi-hard surface. I know that saltwater stays frozen longer than freshwater, from personally testing it. But the ocean is vast and so evaporating saltwater to make salt is probably the best situation for acquiring salt unless salt is already above ground, or above the water table depending on whether people getting the salt are safely tethered, and if they aren't tethered, then they should probably be so, in order to prevent potential sinkholes.

So, my thinking is why not start working on other materials that are less prone to problems like rock walls when building a home. When I traveled to go on church outings some, such as rappelling, I went among some of my siblings, and parents on one occasion where I got to use an 'ascender' so we reverse climbed on a rappelling rope. Such a setup could allow side surface mining of hard rock walling to utilize on a home building project, without digging big holes in the ground, although pond creation may be useful, and better than taking down all the trees on the planet to sustain the ongoing need for refreshing roofing projects from an asphalt sinkhole potential problem to running out of wood eventually when seven billing people, number according to the Chief Intelligence Agency Factbook of planet Earth's population. Now, let's credit earth coming from the first book of the Bible before moving on to the next topic.

I know of additional good climbing walls and that includes one from traveling abroad. I showered some when abroad in areas that weren't hiking terrain. The average shower is "eight minutes and ten gallons of water," according to https://www.energy.gov/eere/femp/energy-cost-calculator-electric-and-gas-water-heaters. Take into consideration most people utilize their water heater regularly costing money and electric power capacity utilization. On safari when I hiked Mt. Kilimanjaro, my siblings, myself, my parents didn't take showers for almost one week. Each aforementioned used antibacterial hand gel. I do like utilizing essential oils, and bought Dr. Axe book about herb mixes that has a handy natural soap formula. When the discussion topic came up about at The Center for Living and Learning about what is a favored hygiene product, I stated, thyme, because the "Herbal Physician Desk Reference" indicates thyme is useful for deodorant. Also, National Geographic states that thymol is a main ingredient in Listerine.

On safari, I got kudu, impala and zebra in Zimbabwe. When I was hunting for the kudu, it was near dusk, sunset, and I got a shot on it after getting off the vehicle, and my nearest age brother said, "Put some more lead in it." So, once the kudu was down in the African terrain we got pictures. I keep the horns at home.

Dad got a cape buffalo, aforementioned wild game, and a wart hog. Eldest this generation brother got same as dad, although he only got what I got plus a wart hog on this adventure, he went back years later for the cape buffalo. Many of got dove and Franklin including myself. The middle brother to me got the same as me, all safari animal taking paid for by dad, but each of us got milk growing, and my twin and myself got good milk instead of the kind that has to be microwaved, so that helped us into Apex, a gifted class during public county school. Point I am making is that us hunters 'brought home the bacon' and weren't showing during plains game hunting.

Being majority English and Irish and to lesser but strong percentages, German, Swiss, and French, according to 23andme.com, where I would hope to connect with my siblings and parents and some more cousins online, because I already connected to a cousin. I had not spent as much time in Africa as the large percentage Africans, albeit having successfully gotten wild game on safari. There are more than one billion Africans, according to the Chief Intelligence Agency Factbook, and that also shows there are about seven billion people globally at about 2010.

College Fraternity lessons

I joined a fraternity my junior year of college, and from my Sigma Phi Epsilon book it suggests (1) not succumbing to vices, e.g., no alcohol, (2) exercising at least 25 to 30 minutes daily, and (3) the ethics principles are as follows:

"Honesty: Be truthful, sincere, forthright, straightforward, frank, candid; do not cheat, steal, lie, deceive or act deviously.

Integrity: Be principled, honorable, upright, courageous and act on convictions; do not be two-faced, unscrupulous, or adopt an end-justifies the means philosophy that ignores principle.

Promise-Keeping: Be worthy of trust, keep promises, fulfill commitments, abide by the spirit as well as the letter of an agreement; do not interpret agreements in a technical or legalistic manner" "to rationalize noncompliance or create excuses for breaking commitments.

Fidelity: Be faithful and loyal to family, friends, employers, and country; do not use or disclose information learned in confidence; in a professional context, safeguard the ability to make independent professional judgments by scrupulously avoiding undue influences and conflicts of interest.

Fairness: Be fair and open-minded, be willing to admit error and where appropriate, change positions and beliefs, demonstrate a commitment to justice, the equal treatment of individuals, and tolerance for diversity; do not overreach or take undue advantage of another's mistakes or adversities.

Caring for Others: Be caring, kind and compassionate; share, be giving, srve others; help those in need and avoid harming others.

Respect for Others: Demonstrate respect for human dignity, privacy, and the right to self-determination of all people; be courteous, prompt, and decent; provide others with the information they need to make informed decisions about their own lives; do not patronize, embarrass or demean.

Responsible Citizenship: Obey just laws (if a law is unjust openly protest it); exercise all" "rights and privileges responsibly by participation (voting and expressing informed views)," "and public service;" "leadership or authority, openly respect..." "and assure that others have the information needed to make intelligent choices and exercise their rights."

Pursuit of Excellence: Pursue excellence in all matters; in meeting personal and professional responsibilities, be diligent, reliable, industrious, and committed; perform all tasks to the best of your ability, develop and maintain a high degree of competence, be well informed and well prepared; do not be content with mediocrity, but do not seek to win "at any cost."

Accountability: Be accountable, accept responsibility for decisions and the foreseeable consequences of actions and inactions, and for setting an example for others. Parents..." "employers, have..." an "obligation to lead by example, to safeguard and advance the integrity and reputation of their families, companies..."; "avoid" "the appearance of impropriety and" "correct or prevent inappropriate conduct of others."

Hiking Mt. Kilimanjaro

In preparation of hiking, each of our family took many vaccinations before traveling. I also walked hills per encouragement. Since then, I researched vaccinations and since I haven't caught any diseases that maybe viral that I seem to have been within proximity, I feel that cooking spit to a boil seems to work effectively in making a vaccine. Higher heat, using natural gas or butane may work even more effectively for more difficult viruses or bacteria, such as prions. Salt may work also in creating vaccines. Magnesium also works in preventing a prion from infecting, according to an article I printed off about the chronic wasting disease (CWD) prion prevention remedy.

Itinerary

JUNE 15, 2005 – Depart
JUNE 16th – Kilimanjaro airport,
Springlands hotel
June 17th – Aclimate, rest, hike (rainforest)

June 18th – Moshi, Marangu Park Gate,
Marangu gate (1980 meters (m))
→ Mandara hut (2,700m)
Montane Forest, 12 kilometers (km), five hours (hrs.)
June 19th – Mandara hut (2,700m) → Horombo hut (3,720m)
Moorland, 15km, 6hrs
June 20th – Horombo hut (3,720m), acclimatization day
June 21st – Horombo hut → Kibo hut (4,700m)
Alpine desert, 15km, 6hrs
21st Eve – sleep approx. 7pm to 11:30, ascent
June 22nd – Kibo hut (4,700m) → Uhuru Peak (5,895m)
[8 hours] then back down → Horombo hut [6hrs]
-stone scree & ice-capped summit
June 23rd – Horombo hut (3,720m) → Marangu gate (1,980m)
-summit certificate: 6 hrs
June 24th – Arusha, Lake Manyara
June 25th – Manyara, Serengeti Nat'l Park
June 26th – Serengeti Nat'l Park
27th – Seronera wildlife lodge (2 nights)
June 28th – Ngorongoro Crater
June 29th – Ngorongoro Crater
June 30th – Ngorongoro Crater

Day 1 (U.S.A.)
Wednesday | June 15, 2005

"We awoke today with the prospect of flying to Tanzania for the challenge of hiking the tallest peak in the continent at 19,340 feet high. My aunt and uncle-in-law picked us up as we each loaded two suitcases filled full of zero degree F rated sleeping bags, electrolyte powders, breathable clothing and numerous items that overflowed to a day pack, which we carry. My father and mother, younger sister and I arrived at the airport with plenty of time to grab a Memphis BBQ before departure. My eldest brother met us at the airport. Each boarded the plane at 2:35pm that would take us to Detroit, then Amsterdam where we would meet up with my nearest of age brother, my twin sister and her husband. Unfortunately, my nearest of age brother's most recently acclaimed wife caught mono so she could not join the adventure. With the eight hour flight to Amsterdam, we arrived the morning at 9:05am on Thurs.

Swahili: Hello = jambo, please = tafadhali, thank you = asante sana, slow down = pole pole, lion = simba, elephant = tambo, beer = pombe, how much mommey? = ngapi?, may I take your picture? = mikipige picha?

Day 2 (Africa)
Thursday; June 16, 2005

We met to gather all party members in Amsterdam before our 8:35 hour flight to Kilimanjaro airport. Sleep was elusive on the plane as we read, I read an interesting historical account of modern finance "The House of Morgan" while the fam and I talked and watched movies. Final arrival in Kilimanjaro occurred at 8:05pm, Kili time. We bussed to our hotel –Springlands—and the family had cheese sandwiches, Kilimanjaro beer..." (I disagree with consuming alcoholic beverage now if access to some means of vaccinating although herbal tincturing may be done utilizing liquor, according to various resources including experience with product from an herbal specialist) "...and water while we discussed the trip ahead, past travels, and enjoyed each others' company.

Tomorrow, we have breakfast, take a jungle walk (3 hrs.) and get ready for our hike up Kili Mountain (Mtn.) to the Uhuru peak after a complete briefing by our guides.

Day 3 (Springlands Hotel)
Friday; June 17, 2005

We awoke to our first African breakfast – cheese omelets, hotdogs, toast, coffee, fruit and juice. Interestingly, we met the mother of some older teens, named Eileen, and their photographer for four of the seven summits.

Following breakfast, we check emails at the hotel then met up with our guide, Lawrence, for a quick three hour hike through the rain forest. We saw a great deal of monkeys – black and white, black and blue – leaping through the trees.

People farmed private plots of rice by hand as we walked across a mud wall through the watery fields about a foot high. We strolled through deep forest with enormous trees by height that were used for making hard wood tables, chairs and firewood. Farmers even said that the acacia tree was a popular tree for cooking because it made good coals – Memphis BBQ.

On our way back we saw birds in the rice fields looking for "small fish and small frogs" to dine on, according to our guide. After stomping across the muddy, thin walking path created by the locals, Lawrence washed our boots. We even saw a dung beetle pushing around a ball of dung; while kids in the neighborhood ran to us and said goodbye.

Upon return to the hotel, we went for a quick swim, packed up our bags and before that met with our "de-briefer" and "guide" – Colorado. We were told about the trip, cleaned up and headed for a dinner buffet, just after grabbing some Tusker beer. Dad gave us Tiffany's letter openers and the girls got powder compacts with our initials engraved on them. The drive was fine, we were sleepy, and ready for bed to make our big start up Kili mountaini!

Day 4 – Madara Hut
Saturday, June 18th, 2005
[Day 1 of hike]

Today we had breakfast, packed our bags and loaded up for the 50 minute drive to Moshi for entrance into Kilimanjaro Nat'l. Forrest by way of the Marangu Park Gate at 1,980m. We trekked our way up to the sign in place and hit the trail that consisted of lava rocks lining the way to the top. The trail was beautiful with trees as tall as the sky, vines draping with waterfalls dispersed around.

Hiking through the "Montane Forrest" was more difficult than expected because the gradient was steep. We had to "polle, polle" or "slow, slow" which is translated from Swahili to English. Stopping for lunch provided a nice break as we filled up with water, ate chicken eggs and little bananas then continued upward. The 12 kilometer hike ended at 2,700 m.

As we arrived, we loaded gear into the A-frames, had tea and coffee, then hiked around the rim of a crater. I was completely exhausted and cold, and fell asleep for a split second standing up. But it was beautiful because I believe we are entering the crest of Moorland. We had a nice dinner, ventured to the bathroom... and went to sleep – at approx. 8:05pm. The temp is about 58 degrees F.

Day 5 – Horombo Hut
Sunday; June 19, 2005
[Day 2 of hike]

We woke up at 6:30am, officially, because the guides came to wake us up with "bed tea." However, we were up numerous times last night because we are drinking 4-5 litres per day plus drinks for breakfast, lunch and dinner. After tea, we ate breakfast of omelets, corn, wheat and hot dogs.

After packing up we trekked through the moorland and spotted limited wildlife as a bird of white neck and lizards. We saw plants such as the St. John's Wart, but more interestingly spotted the third largest peak in Africa – Mawenzi. The brush was shorter and there were a greater amount of boulders along the path with steeper gradient.

Horombo hut, at 3,720 meters 12,250 ft., came within sight at approx.. 5:30/40, and we started at 8:40, so that was seven hrs., but less nearly an hour for lunch and breaks.

Dinner was nice with veggie stew on top, cucumber soup, fried chicken – after popcorn and tea. The toilets were sit-down and porcelain!

It is now 8:24pm. We are about to go to sleep. I am sore, yet rested from last night. Cannot wait for the summit, yet I believe partly what a German told us tonight about the summit – he crawled part of the way to the top.

Day 6 – Horombo Hut
Monday; June 20, 2025
[Day 3 of hike]

My twin sister's extra travel companion of adult age woke up last night numerous times because of heavy breathing, a congested chest, and this morning he had 102 degrees F temperature. However, he joined us for breakfast then we left for Zebra rocks at about 9:30am, after sleeping in till 8:00am (later than usual).

He went back at this point because of not feeling well and the rest of the group went towards "Saddle." Mom ended up stopping early and going back before the top. We went on to the top to see numerous piled rocks. The view was great up here, and sunny. But when we trekked back downward, as well as on the way up, we witnessed an interesting phenomenon as the fog came drifting in swiftly – similar to the movies when the bad guy comes.

We got back around 2:30pm after the approx. 5hr. hike, had lunch of "beef jerky," pancakes and honey, and toast. Following lunch we hung out in Mom and Dads' A frame and my closest aged brother videotaped us – interesting times as we goofed off. I believe this was the 1st time my two brothers, younger sister and I took Diamox to relieve headache.

My twin sister noticed he extra travel friend was feeling bad, still, and nauseous – so she and Dad looked for Colorado and ran into a pediatrician who advised it would be best for him to descend. He did. So did my twin sis – in support of her in-law. They trekked down to Mandara Hut tonight and should arrive at approx. 1:00am."

Since I feel that in order to keep the group together when traveling abroad, each of us probably should have descended among my twin sister when she went down with her male counterpart, I am going to condense the journal for summiting Uhuru Peak paraphrasing, and then restart the journal near when we met again at the Springlands Hotel.

Hiking ensured with no injuries or losses even four of the group achieved reaching the summit and that 50% success ratio for our group is greater than the average 40% success of attempted summing.

I will say, taking a step back near day two of the hike, St. John's Wort (Hypericum perforatum) was found along the way in the mountains of Tanzania, and that an herb that I have noticed sold in America more tropical climate growing. I read about St. John's Wort in a magazine, "Use: St. John's wort is best known today for its use in the treatment of depression...used...to treat mental and menstrual disorders, nerve pain, and stomach ulcers, and topically for the healing of wounds and burns. The oil is then massaged into the skin to relieve pain or made into an ointment and applied to treat wounds, burns, and insect bites. St. John's wort is also highly effective against herpes simplex 1 – the virus known to cause cold sores and fever blisters." (Healing Remedies, National Geographic).

Now that I about it, maybe would be good to plan extra days to climatize and if necessary, descend, and re-ascend. If we had thought about it, maybe we should have walked my sister's friend back down the mountain, let him get comfortable, and somewhere we could come back to get him to return home, after we hiked some more back up to the top of the mountain because my twin sister would have been able to go further up the mountain. Regardless, achievement is sometimes not as important as keeping the group together.

Day 7 and 8 – Kibo and Summit (and/or descent to avoid mountain sickness, Springlands hotel)
Back to Horombo (and/or recuperating)

Tues/Wed; June 21st/22nd, '05
[Day 4 and 5 of Hike, or lower altitude helping elevated acclimatization]

Some of us "awoke today and set off for Kibo Hut at 4,703. The hike was approx. 8 hours long and we stopped along the way for lunch at some rocks on the left with wooden bathrooms on the left. We measure the windspeed at 35 mph on the way up as the weather changed radically from sunny to misty clouds unexpectedly. Upon arriving at Kibo, after trekking through dust clouds, we partook in our last supper after signing in, getting water, and securing our bunks in a room among Doug, Mike and some other guy. Dinner was pasta with sauce (veggie), bread and hot drink-tea, coffee, chocolate (milo-the breakfast of champions); we joked about hazing Nestle if we didn't make the top. Bedtime came at 7:00pm. I slept from approx. 7:30pm to 9pm then had to go to the outhouse, which was to the left and behind the building 75 yards. We were awakened at 11:30pm. I was awake since 9:00pm. After getting dressed – about four layers bottom and five layers top, we were about to depart. My middle brother, however, was outside throwing up. He toughed it out. We finally took off to hike at 12:25am. After some time, we braked, and my middle brother got dizzy, and nearly blacked out. He and Theo with Mom (who went down w/ my middle brother in support of him and also because of being sleepy) went back to Kibo Hut.

We hiked past Williams Point, up into more dangerous boulders, and Pheostine took my pack because he said my steps were too short, also Dad's pack. Dad was tired and slipping some on steps – altitude was tough.

We made Gillman's. (As I type the written journal I wonder what my sibling was doing)

Gilman's was 5685 meters, or 18651 feet. I took another Diamox to relieve the headache that had bothered me for the past two hours. Dad fell asleep sitting up. My oldest brother began asking if we really felt like going, younger sister was silent, Dad was hesitant. I said, "I'm going to Uhuru. It's why we came." Although, we probably should have been down gathering coffee and St. John's wort, and taking that to my sister and foraging for rice for her to eat.

All agreed and we left for the peak, with Pheostine (aka Frosty) encouraging us to go fat and take pictures later.

We walked across a path with ice on either side and I guess the wind speed was 60 mph, as compared to the 35mph earlier. One of the females in the group hyperventilated a little but kept going to the peak and survived.

My oldest brother puked fluorescent lime green I saw, and kept walking. He and Frosty talked, he wanted to keep going but didn't want to jeopardize his health, and so he kept walking to the summit.

More hiking, then finally! The Uhuru sign appeared. I was ecstatic and relieve, and began faster pace towards the sign, yelling, hooting.

We took pictures in the 23 degree Fahrenheit cold; eldest brother holding his condo sign; my youngest sister held up her sister's sorority sign; I held up the Clayton Bank and Trust jacket. We took pics and video.

Hiking back Frosty had us nearly running, and we felt exhausted going to Kibo.

I grabbed some lava rocks (I sent them for return) for myself and for friends.

We got to Gillman's, took a break, and wished for an easier way down. We went down through the huge boulders, then skied the scree, and just wanted off the mountain. It was like skiing double diamonds some without skis.

It took us eight hours going up, and three hours going down the same route [8:25am to 11am-ish].

After resting on the rocks together and falling momentarily asleep, we saw Mom, middle brother, and Theo coming up the hill towards us from Kibo – right next to our huts! We all hugged. Both Mom & middle brother were thrilled we were all seeing one another. Middle brother, was feeling fine.

We had an hour to rest before lunch. I took a 45 minute nap then ate some lunch. Mushroom soup and bread, water, and then downhill to revisit Horombo Hut.

Walking back to Horombo Hut was awful. I was tired, exhausted, wobbly, coughing, nose running and had a sore throat – not to mention – a headache. We traveled down, back down the hills that got us to this hut and mountain in the first place. I double checked with Theo that my side effects were not saying I would have serious problems – he said it was normal.

The hike made running a marathon look like sissy work.

I really think that going up a higher peak would be a waste of time because this peak with the family was plenty – the toughest thing I have ever done in my life.

I was dreaming about having a vehicle pick us up to drive us – instead of walking. After what seemed like another century, Horombo was in sight. We signed in, got a six bed hut, and took it easy for 45 minutes until dinner time. I fell asleep.

Dad and oldest brother missed dinner – nauseous. I ate some rice with Mom, middle bro and youngest sis – fatigued.

Then we slept. Oh yes, we slept long and hard. This was the 1st time in 5 days that I actually got a good night's sleep.

Day 9 – Horombo to GATE!
Thurs, June 23, 2005
[Day 6 of hike]

Waking up, I felt like a new man. With a good night's sleep, at approx. 11 hours (8pm to 7am) we were ready to move towards the gate a t a higher walking pace. Breakfast, packing, then on the road again.

Hiking took us back down to Marangu Hut, where we had lunch. At this point, the fried bread was stomach churning so I whipped out the trail mix, dumped them onto aluminum foil, and picked out the pistachios and cashews. The Kitkat I had saved also hit the spot for my oldest brother, middle brother & I.

We took pics as we walked down the trail under the beautiful, old trees. Discussion between the kids revolved socially liberal viewpoints on marriage vs civil union, abortion & legalization of marijuana. Interesting topics.

Locals sold to us, or tried to sell, t-shirts, maps, flags of Tanzania, and other knick knacks.

When we got to the bottom, we were relieved as we stopped for s, b, and porters.

Theo gave some of us certificates. I got Phaosten's college name, in case I'll put someone through college. We took pics with the certificates, and boarded our bus back to the Springlands hotel.

Arriving at the hotel was great. We showered off the layers of dirt, smell and hair. It felt so good to get clean and to shave.

I took a massage afterwards – right before dinner. This was heavenly – she worked the soarness out of my legs with her hands.

Dinner was good, especially the fried chicken. We drank champagne and ate well for the first time in a week.

I don't drink alcohol anymore, unless tiny quantity percentage-wise to ensure my wits are about me.

Night came and we went for the bed after staying up a little while.

Day 11 – Serengeti National Park
Saturday; June 25, 2005

On the way to the Serengeti National Park from Lake Manyara we stopped for shopping and I bought the flamingo painting. We proceeded to the Masaii village where traditional living coupled with being a tourist attraction. We were greeted by the chief who explained how they still drink blood and milk from the cows, the way of life within the ability to buy wives with ten cows and the dancing and warrior land.

We entered their cow dung/ straw/ stick homes which apparently last three to five years. We jumped with the Masaii. We watched one Masaii build a fire out of no more than a machete, piece of wood and cow dung that ended up in flames.

Then we bought shields, spears, stocks and knives. I bought the machete of the chief.

We entered the Serengeti Park and one of our first encounters was with a pack of lions. It was exciting because they lay abreast the top of an eroded hill – males and females, then walked down to approach our sport utility vehicles – we thought they might jump in to take us as prey.

We stayed at the Loho Wildlife Lodge which was in the kopjes with high ceilings. Middle brother among myself had a Jack and cola at the upstairs bar inside the hidden cave. Again, I don't drink alcohol of that amount anymore, maybe would share one drink among an entire table of four or more.

Day 12 – Serengeti
Sunday; June 26, 2005

We stay at the Seronera Wildlife Lodge tonight for two nights.

During the day we went for a game drive through the Park and witnessed the "great migration." Tons of zebras and wildebeests were gathered everywhere. We saw giraffe, impala, Grants gazelle, Thompson gazelle, eland, a black backed jackal. The drive got me frustrated because I want to hunt. There were approx. one million zebra in the park and 2.2 million wildebeest. We also saw Topi.

We relaxed on the kopjes and were served drinks as we watched the sun set over a huge field with Acasia trees set before us. Beautiful.

Monkeys and Hyrax played and scurried around the wooden frame motel. Dinner was buffet style and we enjoyed each others' company on the lower deck.

We also saw a wounded lion next to a pond and then one next to a zebra which was half eaten and in a tree. They climb trees to avoid the pesky bugs.

Day 13, Serengeti
Monday; June 27, 2005

On the game drive today, we saw warthog, cheetah, leopard, lion, birds, vultures, hippo, topi, giraffe. Two leopards were seen – one was hardly discoverable but the other was a big male who ran down the tree when a troop of baboons began getting close to it. You see, they will team up on a leopard and can sometimes kill leopard.

We saw three cheetah – the first was for in the distance and appeared as just a spot to the right of three impala. The second cheetahs were under a tree much closer. We thought the first cheetah would pounce on fighting Thommys but he must have had his meal for the day, because the guide Mawala said they kill one per day with a 90% success rate and 40% rate of eating.

Saw some ions today, but the highlight was the pit of hippos – one big fat smelly family – over 50+ a croc. They bellowed, wrestled and were just plain ugly. Arriving back, oldest brother and nearest age brother's room got ransacked by vervet (black faced) monkeys! Monkeys entered the room though a window, ate trail mix in the bathroom and turned on faucets then played in the water, left wild insects, and tissues everywhere. The scene was somewhat humorous, astonished that the windows don't have a safety lock, apparatus, or good screen for when open. However, my eldest brother fed one of them two sleeping pills, with unknown outcome.

We met three girls from New York City who planned to go to Kili to hike so we spent some time re-hashing the experience of hiking, in abbreviated version, gave a little warning of how and when to be careful to help safety, and showed a clipping of our success at the summit on my video camera.

After dinner, my two brothers and I had some Grand Monie at the bar then sat on the back porch and spoke with the same girls (two of them). Again, I don't consume alcohol anymore, maybe in tincture form except when mixed with herbs for preserving the medicinal herbs and adequately low percentage level when the dropperful or half dropperful or certain number of drops or teaspoon amount is combined with water.

I went to bed to prepare for the next morning hot air balloon ride.

Day 14 – Serengeti > Hot Air Balloon,
Ngorongoro Crater
Tues; June 28, 2005

We awoke at 5:00am to go on our hot air balloon ride. This was exciting as we met for hot tea and coffee in the breakfast room then rode to a field for air briefing before climbing into the 16 person wicker basket facing parallel to the ground. One pilot filled the balloon with hot air and we began to drag across the ground and into the air.

As we floated approximately 150 feet in the air, we watched as wildebeests make their funny noises and scurry, frightened, away from us blasting hot air. We watched zebra, topi, jackals, impala, gazelle, wildebeest, and hyena 'fanning out.' After about a 40 minute flight, we landed. This involved bouncing approximately four times through the 25 mph wind across the Serengeti. Breakfast – English style – followed a champagne landing celebration. We had toast, eggs, bacon, sausage, beans, fruit and coffee.

Again, I don't drink alcohol anymore, even a glass of champagne, unless maybe I have a stomach infection depending on research I might do to find out what remedy alcohol is.

More recently, post journal entry, while washing potatoes I ate something spicy so I thought about vaccine creation without the help of heat, and thought about pinching spit, a vaccine maybe possible to be created through inactivating a virus or bacteria though that St. Patrick's Day approach.

We packed and drove to the Ngorongoro crater, where a great lunch was served as we ordered from a menu for the first time in almost 1.5 weeks.

Right now, I sit in an inside glass window porch as part of my shred bedroom my nearest ago brother is sleeping off the early morning, long drive and nauseated stomach.

I am overlooking the beautiful Ngorongoro Conservation Area (NCA) which spans 8,300 sq. km. Each of the huts has a view very similar, which are to the left of the backside where the pool and patio rest for the Sopa Lodge.

The view is impressive of the crater, a steaming ice patch in the floor and rift mountain edges. We are positioned on the rift wall, so it is cool and windy. The temperature will fall after sunset due to the elevation.

Our trip is nearly over because tomorrow we spend the whole day on a game drive, followed by one more night here then a brief game drive on our way to shopping and the Impala hotel. Then Arusha and departure.

Day 15 – Ngorongoro Crater
Sopa Lodge
Wednesday; June 29, 2005

Woke up had breakfast buffet style. Cute Spanish girl entertained my two brothers and myself as she gave me a look as I ordered my omelet. Ha!

Unfortunately, my sister's ex-husband (husband at the time), Dad, and younger sister all had diarrhea problems (I later took velvet bean to resolve diarrhea on another occasion post journal entry, also known as Mucuna Pruriens, that I read about in the Herbal Physician Desk Reference (PDR) which made me go 'normal,' and they felt bad so they slept in their rooms while we wet viewing in the park conservation area today. Although my middle brother, Mom, twin sister and I all have diarrhea too. My oldest brother had it last night but is OK today. We must have eaten some bad food at the "English breakfast."

Mawala, our Leopard safari driver, took us into the crater and although we have "been there been that" there were some memorable experiences.

First, we saw cheetah off to the right – two of them close to gazelle, but no attacks. We then saw four lions in the long grass. Quite creepy how they appeared and disappeared at ease when standing and lying, respectively. A hyena came closer we took pics and rolled around in the muddy water.

A pride of close to seven or eight lions and one big black maned lion (very takeable, depending on whether we need to help some of the carnivores depending on intelligence cross analyzed with natural physical advantages of competing animals to prevent excess nitrogenizing soil) rested in the short grass. I add in post journal that for desalinating soil, limestone, 'garden lime' is utilized such maybe good to mix in cattle pasture. My nephews hopefully will get to access some of the area where deer live. I want to provide garden limestone to those who might have too much salt from urine to accommodate residing square footage and to help advise through the grapevine how to work the soil. Maybe I shouldn't put in this book whether or not I have nieces?

We had boxed lunch and the biggest elephant I've ever seen, probably 80 to 100 lbs. per tusk came walking through the park site. We chased. {I add in after journal writing something about risks on urine distribution from larger than humans non-planned on done properly requiring at least garden lime mixture to some fertilizers (see p. 19) due to non-correct amount of salt added otherwise}. A smaller tusk elephant confronted him and he (the big boy) chased the small one off. We saw rhino – completing The Big 5 spotting, and called it a day.

|------Africa End ------|

Bloomberg Interview

I interviewed with Pimm Fox, reporter for Bloomberg TV on December 27, 2010.

I first talked to a Bloomberg employee when a news reporter, Nick Baker called me due to my involvement in the Clayton Homes/ Berkshire Hathaway deal. During a student trip from the University of Tennessee to Omaha, NE, since I had been interning to Jim Clayton, I presented a book, First A Dream, to Warren Buffett when I shook hands with the man and got a picture showing me handing Warren the book and greeting Warren, and that picture got published in the Knoxville New Sentinel. Nick Baker picked up the lead and wrote an article about how I got a letter from Warren Buffett titled "Letter from God" because once the deal was being completed, I asked Clayton to arrange getting me a letter of recommendation. "Don't use the Lord's name in vain" (I sometimes hear from Mom to me who was appointed an elder in a protestant church for a while); God's holy spirit is at work, and our spirits are made in to mimic and honor God and our parents, "Honor thy mother and thy father" (The Bible). So, I spoke with Nick about the deal when he called on the phone.

I am going to provide my interview with Pimm Fox on Bloomberg TV, because I was focused on how to make money in a low interest rate environment. After seeing an interesting chart on Japan real estate values in a Gavkal book courtesy of a friend there while I was working at Davis Selected Advisors, a mutual fund in New York, New York, during 2006, I felt the market was somewhat undervalued.

So, here's a transcript of my interview, that derived from a research note that I wrote inspired by Kyle Bass, who works or worked for Hayman Advisors, a letter that Chip T. emailed to me.

Pimm, "What's happening in Japan, and why should investors in the United States pay attention. Well, we've got Richard Wright with RBW Capital to help illuminate the situation. Richard it's good to have you here on Bloomberg." "It's great to be here." Pimm, "So what's happening in Japan. Alright, we know that there's been a new government that's been installed, seems to be an economy that's in stall mode for many years. Is there a vibrant sector of the Japanese economy that's starting to get going with all of that government stimulus that they've pumped in?" Richard, "Well you're starting to see some of the stimulus flow into real estate and equities. So, the Nikkei 225 which has an inverse relationship to Japan bonds is starting to benefit. So, the Nikkei is at 10,335 and I think as that rises, Japan interest rates at 1.15%, are going to rise in tandem."

"So you think real estate and equities in Japan are going to benefit from various types of stimulus that are already in the system or they're going to have to do even more." I responded, "Well, they're doing more right now. They just decreased the tax rate by 5%. And so that is one of the stimulus. What you're seeing is capital flowing out of the bonds." Pimm, "Because the yields are not giving you anything, right. What are we talking about with yields on 10 year Japan bonds." Richard, "It's you know 1.15%. There are dividends you can achieve higher rates of return on some hotel REITs and certain banks within the environment because the CD (certificate of deposit) rate that they're earning is at .1%.

".1% for a Japanese CD. Why would anybody own Japanese bonds?" Richard, "I can't figure that one out." Pimm, "You think patriotism is a factor. In something that you wrote recently, 94% of all the Japan government bonds debt is held by people or institutions in Japan." Richard, "That is a fact. One of the reasons that has been successful, historically, is because the CPI (consumer price index)/ inflation has been negative 1.1% last year, and so. As prices start to increase on real estate and equities, there's a mismatch. Consumers, local businessmen who would like a greater return on their investment are beginning to sell the bonds that they own." Pimm, "Because they're not getting anything by holding them. In fact, we've got a chart here taking a look at the 10 year yield on Japanese government debt. You can see that it's under 1.2%. So, does this indicate to you that if you're a smart investor, and you can figure out an efficient way to make the trade, you want to be selling Japanese bonds right now. Just as many people in the United States, we've heard Chuck Liberman earlier saying he's already sold all his US treasuries. Sell your Japanese government bonds." Richard, "That's precisely, well, you have about a nine and a half trillion debt to GDP (gross domestic product) ratio at 180%. And so, because of this." Pimm, "That sounds worse than the United States." Richard, "It is. You have a better ratio in the United States. The Bank of Japan is selling. They're doing that to...also sell the yen. And that's having a positive impact on the real estate market. Over a 20 year period, real estate has not appreciated to the extent that it is in today's time."

Pimm, "Do you think that's a lesson for U.S. investors that have always counted on rising prices, inflation in the real estate market because the Japanese real estate market was always in the headlines because of the outrageous prices that were previously paid in the early 1980s, and it hasn't come back and here we are now almost 30 years later."

Richard, "Well, you know, they bought the Rockefeller Center. You see. The CIP in the United States was 3.1% for about if you look over a 70 year period. If you normalize GDP, GDP growth in Japan was 3.9% over a trailing three month period. As that GDP growth attracts investors from abroad into the equity markets there's an inverse correlation between the equities and the bonds. So, if yields go from 1.15% to 6%, up by 6%, 5% and 6% to 7% in the next few years then you're going to have a large capital change."

Pimm, "If you're holding bonds, and you don't sell them then you're going to have a huge loss because your principal is going to get crushed. And then relatively speaking, at least what you're saying for equity returns you could be missing out on all those juicy yields and those capital appreciation from the stocks." Richard, "Right. And the dividend that some of the businesses that you're seeing, price to book ratios, price to sales and earnings are very attractive for a developed market. The savings rate in Japan was historically about 17% to 18%, You mentioned in the late 80s, that has decreased to a figure closer to 2% or 3% on a private standpoint. So, allocating that to get the highest return on invested capital is best suited for, appreciation of, you have capital appreciation in equities and then you also have the dividends."

Pimm, "Is it also because Japanese investors are getting older. And therefore, the 1% yield, or 1% interest that they're getting on investments, buying Japanese bonds is not enough to sustain their lifestyle. So, they've got to search for other things, just as U.S. investors have to search for other things." Richard, "Well, if you look at the GPIF, the public pension funds, they have a 3.4% rate of return requirement that recently got increased to 4.3%. This entity could benefit by reallocating, they have about 70% in bonds, as they put that into emerging markets, developed markets to weight towards higher rate of return investments. Then, that will benefit the population, the local population."

"We're going to have to take note of that. See what happens in 2011. Sell those Japanese government bonds and maybe buy some Japanese equities. Thank you very much, Richard Wright, joining us from RBW Capital Management, appreciate your insight."

I was a little early in my perspective on markets. I have since closed down my hedge fund trading operations, and changed the only private long-term investment, Sumzero, Inc. into individual investors names, which includes myself. I went to watch horse polo among another Sumzero investor. I didn't mention to the Sumzero folk that at least one of my great grandparents had a garden helper go get horse manure for gardening fertilizer.

I probably should have added in that "Blooming stems" of the "Arrowleaf" are "peeled and eaten" (63 Moerman) by the "Paiute" that "generally live in the Great Basin region" according to "Native American Food Plants" (25 Moerman). More importantly, I would add that I don't invest in Japan any more than occasionally eating at a Japanese restaurant, and one reason is I would rather have my money in safer assets such as those of American assets. My assets are currently in United States businesses with the exception of an American Depository Receipt for a Sweden/Israeli company doing ocean wave hydroelectric provisioning.

My second television interview was live while I was in New York City, and Susan Li was live from Hong Kong, so here's that transcript:

March 17, 2011

Susan Li, "Yeah, let's talk about the markets, and joining us from New York we have Richard Wright, fund manager at RBW Capital." "Good to have you with us Richard. A lot to intake right now, if you're taking a look at the markets. Now we just got word of the UN Security Council approving this no fly zone in Libya. We still have the ongoing nuclear situation in Japan. What are you trading on?"

Richard, "Hi Susan, um, I am trading on quantitative metrics for the equities, the relative strength index, you mentioned with the Nikkei down to it's like the 8,880 level I think that will rebuild to levels of 11,000, and with Japan bonds I think that you're going to see yields go from 1.2% up to 3% in the next 12 months."

"Ok, Richard now let me stop you right there. Because you just talked about the Nikkei 225, did I hear you right, you think is going to rally to 11,000 in the next 12 months?"

"I think there's a strong possibility of that. With the billions, hundreds of billions that are flowing into real estate, into buildings, into financial banks there's a lot of upside. The issue is with some of the, there are about 8% of the bonds are held by the banks, along with the pension fund, the insurance companies, the central bank. There's about 25 trillion in debt that is held by, if you look at like the G7." "Ok." "Japan's about $10 trillion."

"Well. So, there is a lot of debt, I understand that the government has spent a lot 200% of GDP. People are estimating that the cost of reparation, and the recovery efforts will cost Japan at least $200 billion dollars. Is that good for the economy, for the bonds, for equities?"

"For the bonds, I've been looking, essentially at the, you look at some of the finance decisions that are made. I was talking with a German finance minister. And he said that, um, I asked if they could hedge Japan bonds, countries can't do that. And so, on an indirect basis they can allocate into sovereign wealth funds, into hedge funds, and these are some of the ways to because there's a variance between if you look at China, if you look at the G20, if you look at France, Italy, and the U.S. with gold reserves , they're putting, they can hedge some of their bond exposure with that type of investment."

Susan, "Richard, thank you again for your insights."

Once again, I do use my skilled analytics on a timely standpoint, and after there was an increase of more than 200% in Japan equities, I had already sold the bank investment that I found somewhat underpriced. I still think government bond yields are low, but I don't invest in Japanese markets, with exception of sometimes eating sushi fish, or rice, and definitely avoid the Japanese plum wine because I had one serving once, and it ruined me for feeling as smart as I am for the next day. That was even after a Japanese hibachi meal on a special occasion. I should have ordered fried bananas, gone somewhere else for real fruit, or maybe a cranberry juice as I sometimes get. I don't drink beverages containing alcohol any more, better to 'whiff' to see if fermented, borderline. For this St. Patrick's Day interview review, I was glad to be working and promoting my market ideas during the day. Although, I would rather keep my money where I trust the most, and that's domestic to Americas.

Fast Company Magazine

I felt honored to be called by a Fast Company Magazine employee due to my involvement in handing to Warren Buffett the business autobiography by Jim Clayton, among honored for so many things, and I have additional stories to describe. The ego building article that occurred while I was earning my Master of Business Administration from Vanderbilt University was due to the Berkshire Hathaway purchase of Clayton Homes, making money more 'liquid' for the largest shareholders, that included Jim. Due to a Fast Company Magazine employee interviewing me on the phone, I would like to add part of the article authored by Jennifer Reingold, "The students were thrilled, although Wright jokes that a proper finder's fee for the deal would have been more like 1%, or $17 million." Each of the students that was on the trip got a Berkshire Hathaway Class B share for Jim selling his and others' interests in Clayton Homes to Warren's Berkshire Hathaway.

Commodity Energy Saving Tips

(1) Unplug or turn off your refrigerator when not needed. Utilize sugars, salt, sun-drying when preserving food, possibly small bucket(s) with a press for preservation. An interesting book is "How to preserve food without canning or freezing," wherein "honey" is utilized in very small quantities to line the inside of a jar to prevent bacterial growth.
(2) Cancel and/or minimize garbage being sent to landfills although the Bible does suggest keep trash away from the house. Therefore, buy things that are

needs to prevent excesses, and compost or throw food scraps out to wild critters.

(3) "Protect them" (Dad) RE: fruit trees I bought and planted to prevent goats from rubbing the trees to death and knocking trees over.

(4) Electric bike, boat, or walk to destinations.

(5) Container/hand wash dishes, laundry, then line, hanger dry or "live dry laundry" (I made up live dry laundry when wearing damp clothes partially at The Oaks Behavioral Health after washing some clothes in the shower.

(6) Don't use air conditioning unless pertinent.

(7) Don't heat the air except for "cooking cakes" (Bible, in reference to particular wheat items and sugar has a lengthy shelf life), inventing ways to better our consumption habits, or survival heat, or investing things we need to survive. Small is acceptable when heating air. Do not heat air beyond what may be easily extinguished or let burn out. Ensure adequate clear of kindling area around anything being heated.

I wonder whether eventual travels to "exoplanets" (Summers et. al.) although exoplanets may be unreachable so maybe there is a similar Earthlike planet with a longer lasting Sun, although maybe the books are doing a best guess, so the goal is to stay on Earth even after expiration of the Sun by using geothermal energy, unless they are wrong and the Sun stays going after four billion years forecasted by "The Book of The Sun," Smithsonian. I think the authors have reasonable knowledge.

Also, cooking meats for sharing may also be useful to make vaccines. Cooking spit for vaccinations may be a norm. Alternative pinching spit maybe works, unknown. Maybe cooking natto, potentially into cake, natto is fermented soybeans that create vitamin K2 that helps prevent osteoporosis, or bone frailty.

(8) Don't turn off mechanized air that is providing oxygen to people when there are people that need oxygen and natural ventilation isn't in place and securely fixed into permanency. Once natural ventilation is secured open and available, ok to turn off mechanization only then.

(9) Drain water pipes during freeze situations (I credit my nearest age older brother for residential design putting me to work on that because I installed flexible water tubes in one area that didn't have plumbing). Now, I think about adding metal conduit for fireproofing/ protecting, with exception of sprinklers. Copper pipes break when a freeze occurs, if water is not drained from them at weak points and solder-points sometimes, and the electricity goes out may cause freezing conditions seasonally in winter. Do not turn water pipes off when there are people relying on the water. When pipes rupture if left on, then simply repair with pex pipe, and make sure to have adequate water for those while water is off for a repair.

One of the Bible's 10 Commandments is "Thou shalt not kill."

(10) Rinse with surface water maybe use healthy cleaners like "herbs" (Bible) via essential oils or grass liquid for scent. Tree leaf tea is good. When I traveled to Indonesia via boat among my ex-wife, I bought essential oils that are used to add scent smell-good. I continue to use more natural things. My ex-wife made it back safely to home from Indonesia, and then at different points from that home, to the United States although we both lived in New York, New York before traveling abroad.

(11) Salt reduces the freezing point of water (internet provides degrees). I consume acceptable salt levels.

(12) Ration self(ves) electricity usage. Some percent of total electricity comes from hydroelectricity, which was 287 million megawatt hours in the U.S. last year, according to eia.gov. Seems wise for people to ration their electricity usage per person, such that in America with 330 million persons (according to census.gov), each may be entitled to approximately .87 megawatts of electricity per person annually depending on additional hydroelectric output from new hydroelectric turbine completions, in addition to other renewables. This includes environmentally friendly "renewable" electricity, listed at 439.8 million megawatt hours, the equivalent of 1.33 megawatts per person. Combined ration at 2.2 megawatts of electricity per year per person.

(13) Use safe natural ventilation. I credit my mother for suggesting opening windows when the weather is nice.

(14) Re-use water when applicable {I credit my middle older brother per boating practice}.

(15) "Let's go to _______'s Orchard" (twin sister to me)

(16) Buy or make or add "cover" (Bible) for sunburn prevention, comfort, and warmth.

(17) I am thankful my oldest this generation brother to me gave to me a photo on how some sun-dried cape buffalo jerky is made on African wilderness safari.

(18) Use cotton rags or t-shirt cloths for wiping, when not having to be ultraquick to accommodate roommate(s), and make sure they are cleaned nicely to ensure roommates or hosts are satisfied with your cleanliness to ensure there isn't a smell and maybe best keep those out of plain sight from others to keep from raising the eyebrows so to speak, and allowed to dry with natural ventilation seems the most sustainable; I got the idea from one of my sister's communication of cotton baby diapers (her and her newly added this generation husband) via my mother's saying that's what she does when I was discussing France using linen.

(19) "Safety first" (director at church camp I worked at near Chattanooga, Tennessee and Rising Fawn, Georgia without experiencing any injuries or losses when teaching high ropes, caving, and kayaking).

(20) Reuse manure and urine to reduce waste loss. My uncle suggested when buying topsoil to "mix it in" with more

claylike soil for root growing capable soil. Manure may be mixed with clay and some fauna like leaf particles to allow for root growth but not too much clay or undecomposed leaves because those are hard for roots to grow in. See the section on fertilizer to know how to distribute urea. (21) Use natural gas instead of uranium for electric power. I hypothesize that uranium is better utilized as a building product, lightning rod, electrical wire, or boat hull.

Trends from eia.gov and a friend's recommendation of the Commodity Research Bureau (CRB) Yearbook have assisted me in typing and writing to improve energy consumption habits after reading a Standard & Poor's energy sector report from the Tennessee Valley Authority (TVA) Investment Challenge. I also find the information on livestock ratios (e.g., cows and goats (plentiful)) and agriculture to be interesting.

Solar utilizing silver data is useful also, at current consumption rates, and taking into account degradation found in Mohile's book, and silver at one ounce per 100 watt solar panel according to a solar panel book I read, at current supply and demand status quo projected out there's about 800 years of silver remaining. Silver is the best conductor of heat according to book *Metallurgy.*

Electric based Needs and Ocean Wave Hydroelectricity:

Take a moment and write down your true needs for electricity. You might be alarmed that all you need to cover such needs would be a portable solar panel set.

Right now, I write that I need electricity for a computer, printer, 20-30 cup hot water heater/ portable coffee heater that I use for warm overhead bucket showering, an eight cup hot water heater for tea/ coffee, phone and maybe an incubator for making natto, maybe natto is a want although food is a need. Some of these may be wants. Electricity is probably only useful for getting seeds replanted and distributed to where we need, and to get mineral nutrients to where we need. We learned at early age that needs are food, shelter, clothing. I would add good morale.

I use the incubator to make natto, also known as fermented soybeans. I could probably make those during the summer using sun-heat, and are those a real need? The problem is, everyone is using an extraordinary amount of electricity including solar, so we'll simply run out of electricity due to the overconsumption habits of everyone within 1,000 years based on my projections depending on whether hydroelectric sources can keep copper and aluminum working much longer. Uranium if can be utilized with ocean wave hydroelectricity could last billions of years. Therefore, if that is possible or feasible then the electric mix must be rejiggered to not use uranium for wants, and that is excess 'easy living' without a needs based approach. Natural gas is the better alternative for cooking and hot wire charging.

Then I will get to make natto if ocean wave hydroelectricity is done correctly, but if we use all the uranium due to enrichers and fusion, then there won't be any winter natto, or winter tanning beds to help us get over a bad night of sleep. This is one of the reasons for this book; to extend the duration of my electric needs accessibility and to help people in jail, get ready and to ensure they have a way out when they deserve fresh air, natural lighting and the ability to plant and work forage, to the extent they rely on needs system and not wants. If you think you need something but really don't, reduce consumption. I could pass up taking a hot and cold water mix bucket shower by using Thyme oil, which I ordered from Amazon.com, and believe thyme to be a good deodorant due to the fact that thyme is glossaried as such in the PDR for herbal medicines.

Problem is people like to use inedible shampoo and soap in the shower which bad for the water. Detergents are bad for the water. Dishwashing detergent is bad for the water. I am thinking about becoming a criminal defense attorney or an environmental attorney.

The Clean Water Act is supposed to ensure water is kept clean, and "the Administrator is authorized to make joint investigations with any such agencies of the condition of any waters in any State or States, and of the discharges of any sewage, industrial wastes, or substance which may adversely affect such waters. (1252 page 332)." The Environmental Protection Agency (EPA) website, epa.gov, discusses the Clean Water Act. Further, "The Administrator shall, after careful investigation, and in cooperation with other Federal agencies, State water pollution control agencies, interstate agencies, and the municipalities and industries involved, prepare or develop comprehensive programs for preventing, reducing, or eliminating the pollution of the navigable waters and ground waters and improving the sanitary condition of surface and underground waters." Some shampoos and soaps are biodegradable. However, a combination of shampoo and soap-water is hazardous as can be seen through a cousin of mine used to drink some of the bathwater when she was even littler than she currently is, and it caused a tumor. Her Dad caught the largest sunfish, setting a record, that got in the newspaper. She took chemotherapy to repair her body to be rid of the tumor, and has always been lively and energetic that I have seen. I feel I might have helped her more healthily if done with herbs, by using Cat's Claw, and the herbal PDR, if I got that to my cousin to help her earlier. I did sell one of the herbal books to him, so hopefully she gets to read the information. My cousin, her Dad, helped supply wild game to his kids from my parent's property where he is allowed to hunt, once he helped show me how to clean beyond gutting get some venison from a deer, and enjoyed some holiday gatherings among him, his family, including his children.

There is a book titled “Essential Oils by Dr. Josh Axe, et. al. which I bought that provides ingredients for “baking soda shampoo” which is defined as “1/4 cup baking soda, ¾ cup purified water, 10 drops lavender essential oil.” Dr. Axe’s ingredient for “dry shampoo” are “two tblspns cornstarch or arrowroot powder, or two tbspns cocoa or cinnamon powder, two drops lavender oil, and one drop peppermint essential oil.” In using banking soda for shampoo as a chief ingredient, it seems to work as a cleaner; my only concern is does it settle and possibly create a drag in the outgoing pipes if used in large enough quantity over a really long time-frame? Who knows, that would be difficult to test, baking soda certainly is a good outdoors shower ingredient, but I would not recommend using it with traditional plumbing when rinsing out the hair if that is ever done with dry shampoo because it settles fairly quickly and could cause plumbing stoppage if in large quantity. I would suggest using the smell good essential oils alone for hair scent when showering indoors on a regular basis.

Pond Creation

Dig a pond, for drinking water and fishing, or install a plumbing connection cut off at ground level for one faucet if you worry about running out of electricity to warm the above ground level pipes from rupturing. You may be able to get a plumbing blueprint of your home from the county clerk.

A friend of mine’s father has access to equipment for digging ponds if anyone is interested in a referral do contact my phone or email me your phone number so I can share your information providing to him for an estimate. Digging a pond by hand is another option, and an uncle to me has dug small waterholes using a shovel. The only issue without fish such as brim are mosquitoes, so that’s why about ½ acre (from internet research is optimal for fish) because they control the laying water area from being mosquito prone.

Salt

Also, something to consider is a saltwater tub. I bought a salinity measuring thing that is made of plastic, from a pet product store, that is useful to manage a body of water’s salt level, to enter, if attempting to achieve semi-permanent clarity to achieve salt level at that of the ocean. I bought an e-book on salt, and apparently plutonium spent waste from satellite imagery consumption is buried deep in salt mines, and I think it may be better to put plutonium waste in more stable grounds maybe using salt as a sealant for the holes plutonium is placed, “Salt” written by Mark Kurlansky. I think salt is especially good for curing animal furs. I won’t forget when my brother showed me a salted coyote pelt, and so when I get deer I salt the fur skin side and also scrape the fur skin according to “Deerskins into Buckskins” written by Matt Richards although I do not take the hair off the fur discussed in the book to make clothes.

Mold Problem fixed with a Remedy

If you don't use air conditioning voluntarily, like me, you might have an experience similar to what I encountered and that is having some mold growth in rooms. One thing is certain, it's good to keep things clean and wiped off, and keep your windows securely opened a small amount for good airflow yet preventing them from someone else opening the windows more than natural ventilation requires. Now, being new to no air conditioning (A/C) (Never turn off mechanized air without supplying natural ventilation), and I added that because at Vanderbilt Psychiatric floor that I was put at when a cop came and cause me to have to stay there, they turned off my a/c so I had to rest in the group room and couldn't sleep good because of the noise. Then someone turned off one of the vents in the group room so I had to make various calls to get the air working again. Completing my being new to no air conditioning, I was unaware that humans could breath in mold spores and get it into their body. So, I got tested by Amen Clinics for mold and was happy to find that after taking cholestyramine prescribed by Amen Clinics, the mold went away. There is an interesting book titled *Toxic: Heal Your body from Mold Toxicity, Lyme Disease, Multiple Chemical Sensitivities, and Chronic Environmental Illness* by Neil Nathan, MD. I got the book for Christmas from Mom to me, of five, and I was helped by the Mold and Lyme sections of the book. The book talks not only about cholestyramine, but states further that activated charcoal helps remediate mold. Simple as that. So don't panic if you have mold in the house, take efforts to ensure it is ventilated and cleaned better, and buy and take over-the-counter activated charcoal while you may need to get a positive mold test for cholestyramine.

How to Save Trees

Leaves seem to be a good mulch. And campfire ash can be a soil amendment as well, but don't burn all the trees because an internet source I found suggested there's only 300 years left of trees (presumably that would be in my point of view with no change in habits from toilet paper, lighting cause wildfires, and construction spending), unless habits change and supply/ demand based on pricing of wood materials should prevent disappearance. That's why I suggest using t-shirt rags (Lowe's sells them) for wiping and wash in separate laundry load because toiletpaperhistory.net suggests the average person uses 100 rolls of toilet paper per year, say 80 years of that, and we're looking at 8,0000 rolls. "It is estimated that a single tree can make 100 pounds or almost 1,500 rolls of toilet paper." So, that's five trees per person per lifetime. Buy or move to an acre of land and own the trees yourself and re-use cotton rage for wiping if you can afford the land.

I completed an excel project of when tree loss becomes problematic from a needs standpoint and that is about 2065 at current toilet paper consumption rates counterbalanced with ocean acidification due to carbon emissions from coal, natural gas, propane and the lower emissions uranium and hydroelectricity. Coal fuel power has been regulatory disallowed to be burned due to highest emissions relative to natural and uranium. Per watt, nat. gas emits more greenhouse gas than uranium, according to the websites I read querying, and uranium is equivalent to hydroelectric power per wattage. Solar and wind are also to consider.

Plus, tree pricing is going up, as lumber has risen from $.60 cents a board foot to $1.11 a board foot during 2021. A 12 inch tree contains 70 board feet, according to extension.psu.edu/valuing-standing-timber. Give trees is 350 board feet at $1.11 that's more than $350 dollars worth of tree, up-priced otherwise. There, I've saved you that money by buying this book if you simply use white t-shirt rags instead of toilet paper. Toilet paper is bleached and I hypothesize maybe if wiped, rubbed habitually with toilet paper or other paper potentially may cause cancer because I read online dry cleaning is a cancer causer. Please buy more of this book and buy this book for friends and family, because I may use the money to buy food and maintain housing residence and if I have to pay taxes then I'll plan to do so to maintain legal.

Willow tree twigs are utilized to make Aspirin, according to The Druids Book of Medicinal Tree Medicine, so don't buy too many of this book because I need to have some trees living.

Fertilizing

One Christmas Eve, I gave out brand new galvanized cans about three-gallon size, they had lids, to my siblings and some cousins because I had been using such for poo poo to put under tree leaves near the tree trunk. I should not have done so because parental guidance was against give the metal cans. I should have at least added the Humanure Handbook by Jenkins since I bought multiple copies of the book because it outlines how to compost the poop that comes from humans eating normal healthy food. I thought about adding that so they wouldn't be confused as to why I was giving out a mini metal can. Always good to add instructions if there is uncertainty of the use of something. A better object is a screw lid container, such as with mixed nut container at groceries, because smell is contained, although push on top works better when there is freezing temperatures outside. I plan to buy those, or make comparable from nature and forage, and give them out at Christmas with my book that should quote Jenkins' book and paraphrase. Essentially, he mixed poo and urine and grass and then build a containment using crates then stirs occasionally with a shovel and once it gets to a predetermined heat level the pathogens are destroyed and the compost is ready for garden use. If a hole is dug, then a garden calendar by bwi, Top Notch, calls it a "hotbed" for plant growth during the winter when using compost.

Food, and food waste can be composted for fertilizing crops which cleanses the material of pathogens and makes it healthy nutrition for plants. The book *Humanure Handbook* discusses ways to manage peoples' manure, that supplements nutrients for food growth, and crops may flourish when used correctly. This should be done on a small scale, because humans' manure can combust if at a heap that's too large say beware more than ten foot by ten foot, exact dimensions provided in the *Humanure Handbook,* 3rd Edition. Keeping those nutrients from being lost into a giant disgusting cesspool that is mixed with all sorts of toxins is best. Replenish what you take from the soil by properly recycling your poo back into nature. If you don't have any bad pathogens, get tested annually to be sure, and I would suspect putting your poo at the base of a tree out of plain sight probably is good. "Hotbeds" are a good way of compositing in a dugout dirt, or clay hole, which warms. Don't get seen defecating or urinating by the wrong people because some people would try to persecute you for exposure.

Steven Buehner suggested that to prevent plagiarism, one must utilize a certain number of words of a book or other writing material. He also stated in Herbal Antivirals that elderberry is remedy to Covid, pink berry plant 'early shoots' are remedy to the acute immunodeficiency virus, and ginger is remedy to salmonella.

Add in: Fertilizer, according to www.sciencetimes.com, from urine to properly fertilize for one acre, or .40 hectares, according to a Google conversion, is 15,000kg x 2.2 = 33,000 pounds. Although, I feel this is questionable, due to a previous source suggesting that, and I computed based on other use, 1,000 sq. ft. in a garden uses one days worth of human urine. Urine converts to ammonia after 24 hours. Urine is 95% water according to eartheclipse.com while 5% is creatine, electrolytes, pigments, hormones, amino acids, and metabolites, salts and other less able to be consumed products. Seems that once evaporates salt stays while ammonia evaporates, accordingly, "...high concentration of the mixture of salts, urea and creatinine in the urine. In contrast, for a low evaporating condition, the pH of the urine increased to 8.9, which indicates early urea hydrolysis, causing an offensive odor and ammonia loss to the air." (pubmed.ncbi.nlm.nih.gov) I think it important to understand that salt would have to be mitigated because salt has the capability of killing crop and making it unable to grow, my hypothesis, that's why limestone is useful for mixing with such salted dirt.

While at The Center for Living and Learning, I read a New York Times newspaper article titled "Needing Russian Fertilizer..." that suggests "The United States imported $1.3 billion worth of fertilizer – mostly in the form of urea and urea ammonium nitrate – from Russia..." to "supply nitrogen..." (by Kevin Draper B3). I have been thinking about creating a market at my parents to buy my siblings manure and urine separated, although "The Humanure Handbook" by Jenkins suggest keeping manure and urine together—I thinking urine should be separated because of the salt content. So, is urea de-salted? I may study.

Minerals may be found in Bloomberg's BMAP feature, where mined goods are found on a Bloomberg terminal, and also accessible through the B-Unit accessibility feature. Fertilizers also discussed in the Commodity Research Bureau (CRB) Yearbook. I recommend buying the CRB book for studying because that and the World Book Encyclopedia have good information, and The Bible is a first must read, suggesting to "replenish the earth" (Genesis).

Jail Survival

I have been to prison, unwillingly, and that kept me from providing for myself and my family. Jail scares me because people are paid to put people in prison and I don't like one-sided metal door locks.

The time I spent in jail was terrifying. I have been in solitary confinement, in Santa Monica, California. I went to jail in Santa Monica because I thought I wanted to do my best trying to get the person, my ex-wife Anne, to come with me back to a house that she would be welcome, and I should have just made more trips/journeys instead of risking getting in trouble by breaking a French door, that I paid later in court to have repaired although I had enough cash to have it fixed on me when entering, since the doors and windows were closed because she was indoor, where I said "There will be earthquakes! Come with me I have a home that's safer" where she lived with another guy and she came out to the front yard with me to near my car, but then she went back indoor and the cops showed and arrested me. I know from reading that Santa is Latin. While I was in jail in Los Angeles, because I fought two of the four police officers and a security guard when they came and got me in the night in the Santa Monica jail and took me to a hospital, they injected me, asked me if I wanted to stay in the hospital, my reply "Wheel me down by the tree." When I awoke in Los Angeles jail, they never once let me use the phone to call my family. They put cottonseed oil in the peanut butter for the Los Angeles prisoners. I only got to use the physical, in-person visitation and court phones to talk to attorneys and family. One of my siblings had a tough experience while I was in jail, and if I hadn't gone to jail my future would be better. Once I was bailed out, I was scared about court, so I hid my car on a riverbank with two wheels half into the river and the other wheels hardly in the water with the kayak in it, and that was hard to get the car, and the tow people kept my kayak that was now the river's kayak. I was not in the vehicle, no one was in the vehicle when the car got stuck on the edge of the riverbank. I don't recommend doing that, they simply wanted me to go to a mental health facility, so I did that after court got pushed thanks to my self-invented 'extenuating circumstances' (internet search after the fact). While at the mental health facility I read *Edible Wild Plants* and found that corn is high in niacin. I also read *Niacin, The Real Story*, and found that Niacin and vitamin C go good together and are healthy. I went to a mental health facility in Memphis, TN and attended sessions for a couple years then the case was dismissed and expunged.

I was bruised by the police during an escape attempt in Memphis, TN because I was accused of breaking a hair coloring salon shop window owned by a Honduran in Memphis, TN. After a year at a mental health facility in east Tennessee, I paid restitution for the window, and the case was reduced.

While participating at a behavioral health facility in Sevierville, because of a Honduran hair salon window they accused me of breaking in Memphis, and putting a screen on; I was reviewing a section of this book among a female, and I held "Nutrient Power" by Dr. Walsch and a guy asked her to go somewhere so she left, then a staff said they wanted to talk to me at the nurse office. I went there and a cop handcuffed me and took me to a hospital in Sevierville, and they took my clothes and I was wearing a blue paper outfit. I escaped, ran to the exit doors and slept in the woods. Then, I got chased by a group of five and a dog and I got away. Miles down the road near the interstate about seven or eight cops chased and one tazed my while I was running and that caused me to fall down a hill and they came and got me and took me to jail. My parents came to get me again, thankfully. The behavioral health place had to mail to me my house and car keys, my book, and my wallet.

In Knoxville, TN I was bitten by a German Shepherd twice, once on the calf of the leg that left a small gash, and another on near the hip. So, when asked by ambulance folk where bitten I had to pull my britches down some to show where, then I tried to run and my pants fell while cuffed and so I fell and they caught me. One guy broke my pinky finger when originally taking me after the dog bite. I was taken to a mental health facility for a few days, then back to jail, then I went to a Colorado mental health facility for months, and did additional mental health activities for a year and the case was dismissed.

In Collierville, I was followed by a cop into Memphis because he said I didn't give adequate room when I pulled into an intersection, although there was no incident. That cost me because Office Faulkner maced me after the second cop he called broke the driver side window then they pulled me out onto a bridge and four cops were there to arrest me. The reason for my warrant was a filling station attendant was not at the registered and I was charged with entering an amount on the computer then pumping that amount less than $40 in gas into the vehicle I drove, while the attendant came out with a gun to pursue me, and I drove off. I offered him $40 later and he said it's okay, I thought he meant I didn't have to pay him, but then a cop that looked foreign to the U. S., got my car plate, and seemingly reported me. Once in the holding cell, I tried to escape through a ceiling and my shoulder got separated and I had to go to the hospital to get my shoulder put back into socket, plus my wrist rebroke and my right pointer finger broke when I fell through the ceiling panel. My parents came to court and my dad paid the filling station representative, so that charge was dismissed. My resisting arrest charge that's a misdemeanor, is supposed to be dismissed relatively soon.

I then drove to a city in Texas a little later and left some groceries at someone's apartment that I met in Destin at the brokerage office. On the way back I got pulled over for said exceeding the speed limit and was let to go, continuing driving I used my blinker at a stop light but then two cops were following me and so I turned into a Dairy Queen and they came after me said I didn't use my blinker and arrested me in a small town in Emory, Texas and dragged me into the street and had a female sit on top of me. They charged me with bribery because I asked if they wanted me to buy them anything from Dairy Queen, a franchisor owned by Berkshire Hathaway. My parents had to come to get me, released on my own recognizance after 10 days for supposedly not using a blinker! Before that, during the 10 days in prison, all I ate was chips because the food was bad except on some occasions when I noticed good visitors, or workers. The tea was bad too. I also flushed the sandwiches that had bad bread and bad meat in Emory, TX at the prison. Although, the sausage one night was good and I wondered if someone else was going to eat some of the sausage so I didn't eat all of the sausage, and so were two egg rolls, good cabbage. Fortunately, there was a phone in my jail cell and so I got to call my family to pick me up and spoke daily on the phone. My blinker charge and bribery of a sandwich charge was dismissed and I was released to my parents.

When the cops arrived at Vanderbilt Psy., that kept me there because they injected me. They turned off my in-room air conditioning, and so I argued about that about twice a day I would try and get them to turn it back on otherwise I had to spend time beside the hall to get ventilation from there or the group room. The food grease, and oil, and fry part of food was bad in the cafeteria for Vanderbilt Psychiatric floor, so I dipped my food in a water cup or bowl to get the oil off. I was released to my parents.

I am glad to be alive.

I am thankful for the fact that the U.S. has a bail bond system, and I am thankful for therapy/ counseling/, psychiatrists/ nurse practitioners, sensible court participants, and I am thankful for attorney representation.

I am also thankful for work.

If you ever consider doing anything illegal, I recommend researching the penalties before doing any such action, and never consider that it's worth jail time. Because eventually, consider this, if the electricity goes out in jail permanently, you're stuck and probably dead eventually if the generator doesn't properly back up the electricity or maybe lucky if they are required to let people out but there isn't any natural ventilation in jail which is a problem so they should have to grow plants and open the thick plexi and glass windows. There are always better alternatives than doing anything that would cause you to initially go to jail. You may have to read to get such ideas, or talk with someone to brainstorm alternative solutions. We must work to keep each other in better places than jail.

This is why I was considering law school. Bail bond companies give hope and at least temporary release from a terribly awful system.

Work Experience

I am getting paid to help garden. Somewhat recently, I have been using machinery to move pallet of stone, for building, at work. I have worked in sales of solar panels in TN because I considered putting solar panels on the Kroger parking drive where fewer people usually park relative to most frequented in the parking, so further away from grocer customer entrance. At Kroger I packed fresh shrimp, made crab dip, stocked meat and seafood department. At Walmart before that I completed grocery stocking and pet food stocking and felt like I had stock, but in real estate law, it has to be equal ownership for an arguable stake; therefore, owning stock is really just an invitation to attend the annual meeting. I got fired from Walmart by a Chinese manager for planting blueberry bushes near the garden center that I had bought when I was on break. At Lowe's home improvement store for three months part-time I was a sales associate, sold appliances, got appliances down with a ladder, restocked inventory, pulled inventory forward, assisted a cash transaction per and with a colleague's direction, answered plumbing questions because that was the department to which I applied, competed a tree pre-sale for Christmas décor, answer customer calls. At J&M ATV Supply from 2019 to August 2020, I stocked inventory, repaired tent, wrapped tires, boxed supplies for mailing, labeled inventory, recycled cardboard. I worked as an independent contractor recycling cardboard at Pratt for J&M ATV starting in April and continued that after working for J&M, for $20 per pickup, and I delivered more than 3,000 pounds of cardboard. As planter, investor, and renovator from February 2015 until the present I planted over 260 fruit trees, performed three residential renovations, and fully plumbed a garage beside my parents' house.

Entrepreneurially, I ran a hedge fund in the United States from Jan '12 to Feb '15 as the Chief Investor, performed all roles of the fund management, distributed funds and stock. Before that, I lived in Singapore and researched stocks while abroad from July '10 to Jan '12 because my wife got reassigned to continue work for a retailer there where I also met with industry professionals including Jim Rogers. From Nov'06 to Jan. '16 my role was managing the investment fund with focus on buying and selling stock in companies, commodities, and currency, performing marketing activities including research sharing for attracting clients and prospects, interviewed on Bloomberg television, and was published in acclaimed newsletter by respected Economics writer in Oct. '09. I am invested in Sumzero.com to the tune of more than I wish I had invested, which would have better to have been nothing, I should have invested in a company car, and drove away from Manhattan with my wife when her public company offered her a job in Singapore.

I did go out to dinner, since I shared office space among a famous scientist's grand nephew, invited him and one of my wife's friends who read a Bible verse at the wedding, the four of us went out to eat at a restaurant. I rented office space from a professor at a University in New York City, and before that rented office from someone who knew a Memphian that roomed among the NYC mayor, so I talked to him when I visited Memphis because he worked at the company my father worked when he dated my mother as a bond salesman for Morgan Keegan.

I worked for Davis Selected Advisors in 2006 from March until the end of October as a research analyst. I read annual reports wrote summaries of books, wrote appraisals of businesses and summaries of financials, and practices proxy voting recommending.

While at Clayton Bank and Trust I was a Vice President, Mergers and Acquisitions, in Knoxville, TN ending in Feb. '06, and I began as an intern for Jim Clayton in Dec. '02 by picking up boxes of *First A Dream*, the first edition early in the morning, an autobiography by Jim Clayton and delivered boxes of books to his home office, then I helped with bank acquisitions after he sold Clayton Homes to Warren Buffet's company, growing by three banks, managed a bank investment fund for the trust department, then installed automated teller machines.

Before that I worked for the Southwestern Company a salesman and independent contractor in Springfield, MO, after doing sales school in Nashville, TN, during the summer of '02. I completed all sale, ordering, delivering, and accounting for $27,000 in sales during when I prospected, approached and presented 30 sales presentations workdays in eleven weeks, and earned "Gold Seal Gold Award" for working 80 hours per week.

Prior to that in the summer of '01 at Camp Lookout as adventure staff in Chattanooga, TN, and Rising Fawn, GA I taught kayaking on Hiawassee River, caving, high ropes course, and became a certified lifeguard.

In the summer of '00 I worked at the Holiday Inn Select as a front desk agent in my hometown, Memphis, TN. There I checked people into reservation, booked walk-ins, and told people about accommodations.

Education

At the University of Tennessee, I earned a bachelor of Science in Business Administration in Knoxville, TN during May of '03. My major was in finance. I was a value fund research presenter for University's Tennessee Valley Authority Investment Challenge and member of a usual nine members team that earned 48% in three years. I earned a degree from Vanderbilt University in 2005 with a concentration in finance and an emphasis in business law while. While serving as the president of the TVA Investment Challenge in 2004 our team had 20% returns. I also earned a diploma at the Graduate School of Banking in 2006.

Marathoning

During business school I was at a super bowl party with some friends. One of the guys told about completing the Chicago marathon, and I said if you do the marathon I'll do the half marathon. Well, he didn't do the full Nashville marathon but I went ahead and completed the half marathon. For training, I spoke with a classmate in the Vanderbilt TVA Investment Challenge who had completed the whole marathon and I asked about his experience; he described various training courses which I found online and began training. This helped me to successfully complete the Nashville Music City marathon in 2004.

I later moved to New York City for about five years and ran the New York City marathon, and I was happy to see my parents that came up to watch the marathon at about the 16 mile marker and then again at about the 22nd mile marker. At about the 18th mile marker, I stopped and stretched, and then my pace was then much slower when I saw them at the 22nd mile marker. I suggest not stopping and stretching during the course, only stretch before and after a marathon. I was also delighted to see my girlfriend for my first marathon completion. My entry was paid through my parental's donation to Team World Vision, a charity supporting entrepreneurs in third world countries.

The reason I moved to Singapore, where I completed my next marathon, was because my girlfriend who was at the New York, NY marathon that became my wife, got re-located for work with the retail company for which she worked, to Singapore. So, I went with her. While training for the Singapore marathon, I ran outside some around Istana, which was near where I lived and that was the work grounds of the Prime Minister of Singapore and was mostly fenced so I ran along the sidewalk and sweated profusely because it was typically around 80 degrees Fahrenheit. I reduced my time of completion by about an hour running the Singapore marathon.

Planning to make and utilize for water porting a "buckskin bag" (63 Moerman) mentioned in Native American Food Plants since that was mentioned by "Thompson, Southwestern British Columbia" (26) for water, maybe shoes, moccasins, eventually.

After I returned to Memphis, unfortunately by myself, because ex-wife wanted to get divorced when in Singapore after she got a job offer in Hong Kong, I said "I don't want to go to Hong Kong," then I was in trouble with a wife to me.

Before I detail my situation, some research for justifying not wanting to go to Hong Kong read years later, I looked up that there are seven and a half million people in 426 square miles or 3.7 feet per person or 3.7 feet per person, according to Yahoo.com search Hong Kong census and statistic department, so that's cramped. Hong Kong consumes 145 pounds of fish and seafood per person annually, according to www.worldpopulationreview.com, converted online. Getting back to when I was surprised that the public company invited a wife of mine to Hong Kong, I had visited a skyscraping hotel in Hong Kong previously, and because of the excessive density, I didn't want to go to Hong Kong. My ex-wife then wanted a divorce, and she wanted even worse when I declined to going with her to Hong Kong for her job, I doubt she meant what she said, she said "leave," and I figure she was frustrated and mad about the pending separation, and a job in Hong Kong that she apparently accepted without conferring with me beforehand. I didn't want to go to Hong Kong even though I talked about maybe being able to work for a writer there, that works out of Thailand, and is from Switzerland. I met with that writer at a New York City business newspaper event. I don't know whether that Swiss writer is or isn't hiring in Hong Kong, I was only thinking about working for him but I hadn't applied and if I was going to do so, that probably would have been out of Thailand, or Singapore, or United States, but I would prefer working from near where I was born and that's in America where my family is located, or working remotely, I could work for someone anywhere if doing so only using electronics, moving product potentially, and mental strengths.

I should have been trying to get her to move with me back to America afterwards, but she seemed to be staying with her work commitments. I wish I had talked her into coming with me back to America instead of allowing her to go to Hong Kong for a work offer. She came back to America but it took longer than my return to America. Anyways, I ran the Memphis marathon and some of my hometown half marathons. I had a great time jogging, but when I ran one of the marathons, soon after my parents saw me complete the marathon, they went and saw my twin off to be married again while I was deer hunting after the marathon completion and I didn't even get invited to the wedding. I always am happy to see my siblings, and I hope likewise. Most of my planting was so that my twin sister would have an orchard to visit because she wanted to go to an orchard, when I had gotten home to my parents, and she was living about 30 minutes driving time away.

Planting

When I returned to Memphis I was soul searching and so I thought back to an old New Year's resolution I stated in Colorado on a high school aged (for me) family ski trip. That resolution was to read the Bible cover to cover. So I did. One of the books of the Bible was inspiring to me, Leviticus; namely, the discussion on fruit trees. I also heard about some relatives who had planted fruit trees, and upon visiting my sisters I saw from one many indoor plants, and from the other a good outside garden. I am proud of my sisters for growing plants that are edible and breathable. You more outside plants, nearest age, more indoor plants. So, I started planting fruit trees, and have now planted probably 250 fruit trees in Tennessee. I am thinking about growing wheat at the farm of Sanga Creek and indoors if indoor irrigation. I have harvested apples, pears, peaches and figs, although many of the trees haven't grown fruit yet.

I have also done some gardening and been successful with radishes and pumpkin and various kitchen herbs. Daniel Amen MD's book "The End of Mental Illness" discusses that herbs help to reduce free radicals. I have also planted rhodiola, ginseng, and have successfully grown gingko biloba trees from seed.

Root cellars, if the roof can keep it dry and is well ventilated.

I planted thyme, listed in the Herbal Physician Desk Reference (PDR) to remedy a "cold." "Thymol is a potent antiseptic and one of the main ingredients in Listerine mouthwash" (12 *Healing Remedies* National Geographic). I facilitate natural mushrooms and lichens to grow. Mushrooms are an anti-tumor according to "Healing Remedies" (45).

Fishing

Fishing in Florida coast and deep see was much fun; my sisters and brothers and parents all caught fish, and even my ex-wife/girlfriend at the time went fishing and caught fish on another occasion. We went trout fishing, and I caught a brim in North Carolina when renting a house.

I caught an estimated two to three pound bass at elderberry pond in California that sat a tow lot and went bad in Santa Monica, CA. I went fishing in the upper catchment water reservoir in Singapore and didn't catch any fish.

In Tennessee I caught catfish and brim growing up in Cordova on the lake. When I was at home from elementary school, I made a bread trail from the lake into the house that grot ducks into my parents' home, I had to let the duck out after closing the door once they entered. I caught bass going to the farm among my parents, and my brother. Dad has fish in the ponds at the house and we usually catch and release those. I have spotted gar fish on a river in Arkansas when me and my siblings and our parents paddled the river. Me and my twin caught crawdads with our fingers at Gunner's Pool area and on the riverbed there.

I caught trout in Colorado among my Dad and brother.

One of the best fishing trips was when I was 13 years old went shark fishing off the coast of New Orleans, and our boat including my brothers, Dad, and Grand Daddy caught three or four sharks that came into the boat that weighed about 125 pounds each, more than me at the time.

Hunting

Hunting was fun growing up. I got dove, even my youngest sibling got a thrill of showing off a dead dove, saying, "I've got a dead bird in my hands." We used to eat dove with gravy and biscuits that were a fulfilling meal.

I got my first deer in Alabama, and it was a young deer and I was young, old enough to have passed the hunter safety course.

I got a buck deer when my parents went to Hawaii, and on the youth hunt among Grand Daddy, I got a five-point buck. I have hunted deer, turkey, ducks, and geese in Tennessee. The many ducks were gotten at the Frenchman's Bayou in Arkansas among my brothers and Dad. We spent cold mornings breaking ice to show landing spots. Deer were gotten at my parent's farm in TN. I got a turkey because they reintroduced turkeys in TN, and I was hunting at a distance to a friend from high school; his father opened a gun and clothing store, and I got the first gobbler of the farm of my parental's, and parent to me was also there. I got a bunch of ducks after I was dating a female that I met outside bicycling who was walking to a gas station in Collierville, and who saw the fox hunt painting at my home in Cordova, and said "I want to go hunting" so I went hunting and brought ducks to my parents. I also got a goose.

Traveling out of home area to hunt, on safari, I went to Zimbabwe among my sibling and our parents. We slept in thatched huts, and had hot breakfast including fried green tomatoes. On the hunt I got a kudu, a zebra, and an impala. Dad and Larry Jr. hunted cape buffalo, then joined our hunt. We even went on night safari, and a wild cat was gotten by my brother Larry Jr. In the morning, we were awoken before sunrise typically, and brought hot tea with milk before getting ready for the hunt.

When I got an elk my heart was pumping, because it is a huge majestic creature, and there were a bunch of elk maybe 15 to 20 in the herd, and I shot the largest bull, male, at five by six antlers on each side, or 11 total points in Colorado on a hunt among my brother and father.

When we hunted dove in Cordoba, Argentina, I got more doves in a day that I ever got in a single day! We ate dove and orphans got dove donated to them to eat. We ate at good restaurants of beef, bought leather coats, visited Iguazu Falls and had a tango lesson at a fine hotel that was once a family home among my siblings, parents and some in-laws.

I even hunted goats, that I was planning to milk that I bought because when I was in Singapore I went to a goat farm and they kept the goats in concrete stalls. Since I wanted to fulfill a post engagement discussion about money on a house, my mother helped buy a house for me, also so did Dad. So, there was a Japanese maple out front of the house that I didn't want the goats to eat, so I butchered the goats because they kept cutting with their horns the plastic fencing. I should have probably used metal fencing and then they would have probably not been a problem. The goats rubbed the fruit trees that weren't protected so I bought metal mesh fencing to protect the fruit trees, and used metal posts to keep them from ramming the fence down to eat the fruit tree leaves. The goats ate my rose bushes that I planted. Roses help a cough get better according to the Herbal PDR. So, I guess in some way it's a competition of food, and I didn't want the goats out-eating me. I did learn from the goats, and tried eating more leaves and researched eating leaves because the goats ate some leaves and grass. I think I may want to eat some grass, that isn't sprayed by herbicides, since the goats do eat grass, although maybe grass is better boiled or cooked in an "earthen oven" as depicted by some Native American tribes in Moerman's book. A female friend that I met who was Spanish Mexican wouldn't even eat the goat meat because she didn't like goat and her father raised goats in Mexico.

Travel and Adventure

I was born and raised in the United States of America.

When I was about age five, my first snow skiing was at snowshoe mountain in West Virginia where I learned the pizza pie style of snow skiing among my twin sister, brothers, and parents. Ski-in ski-out was an option at one of the places we stayed, so we kept our skis in the lockers.

I learned to water ski at a young age among parents' friends and their family. Me and my siblings used to have tubing battles behind the boat. I learned to slalom at a young age among safe family friends.

I grew up beside a lake and we used to pontoon boat using electric motor because gasoline motors were not allowed. I have a scar from stopping the boat from hitting the dock hard when I put my hand on the dock and the pontoon pinched my hand between my thumb and pointer finger, so I had to get about five stitches, and it didn't hurt, just bled some. I have been to the Kentucky Lake among my twin sister and a couple of friends she invited, on to a pontoon boat that our family had a share invested in the boat within a share of a lake house.

I have visited Colorado snow skiing probably a dozen times, and I have fun skiing double diamonds, and back bowls. We would typically ski, then meet up for a late lunch at a multi-buffet restaurant lodge. We usually brought sandwiches, and would buy extra food because of the exercise we got after breakfast.

We usually skied until the lifts closed at four in the afternoon. Then we would either go back to the lodge and make dinner from groceries we bought that usually included pasta, or more frequently we would go out to a restaurant. One place in Breckenridge offers sea bass that is cooked on a cedar plank that is the best fish that can be gotten from a taste perspective.

My favorite dinners were at Keystone mountain. We would take the gondola up to the big timber lodge, and eat fondue that started with cheese fondue, then would have seafood and 'turf' fondue, and finished off with the best chocolate fondue you could ask for. Warm and toasty and full, we would night ski down, enjoying the swishing of the skis with lighted and groomed slopes.

I snowboarded a couple years when 12 and 13 years old and learned to do jumping 180s and could ski blacks on the second year trying snowboarding trip. My siblings are all good skiers and we enjoy very much skiing the woods on the greens among our parents.

I went dog sledding among most of my siblings, my friend that is my ex-wife currently, and also among my parents. My twin didn't go dog sledding so I probably should have skipped the dog sledding because why fund dogs I don't like dogs anymore. I had fun riding behind a group of dogs pulling the sled. It would have been more fun if all of my family went for the outing. We continued skiing among my twin after the day excursion.

Makes me want to learn clothes making, using cotton seed. I have picked cotton. My mother picked cotton when she was a little girl.

I have more good skiing stories among my sibling, our parents, and even invited friends in Jackson Hole, Wyoming. We played pool in at a country western venue, and went out to nice restaurants. And we skied the slopes at Jackson Hole near the hotel my father's company managed that my brother found.

The most dangerous food I have eaten maybe is cobra snake when I visited China among my parents and siblings, because we spotted it live in a cage on the sidewalk in a major city in China. After China (Beijing and Shanghai, Yangtze River Cruise, silk factory, Comoran fishing watching, tributary boating among my siblings and our parents), we had a flight out of Hong Kong (among my siblings and parents for two days) and got to eat American fast casual restaurant burgers, before heading back to home.

I visited Mexico (my parents went to Acapulco, I visited Puerto Vallarta during business school among nine B-school friends), The United Kingdom, England (London for a Bloomberg conference at the Barbican theatre and also to meet a Financial Times book author then five family office intros on another trip and for an art show), France (Paris among siblings and parents where we say a play at the Red Light district and people undressed behind a screen that allowed us to see only their silhouette), Estonia (among brother and one of his friends via hydrofoil where we walked the town after an outdoor café where my camera was stolen by walkers by), Russia (Moscow and St. Peterburg, the Red Square among siblings and parents where I bought a travel chess set), Italy (ate five and seven course meals among my immediate family (sib's and parents), Germany in 1994 among 14 European countries (including the city of Munich, Neuschwanstein, restaurant Hofbräuhaus notable where I ate big cut of pork that was bone on, sibs & parents), Austria-Hungary (sibs & parents), Czech Republic (Prague disco dancing and absinth trying at an outdoor table among my sibs. & parents), Switzerland (Wengen got into an ice melt lake, and hiked the alps and Zurich, and played full size chess with pieces you walked from one chess square to another among sibs & parents). We went Swiss army knife and watch shopping, and I remember the knife well that was left at the airport, upon request of staff, when I traveled to Singapore because I cared more about the person I was traveling with than the inanimate object. I enjoy hiking and enjoyed visiting the various homes, castles, hotels, cities and wilderness views.

Among some church friends, I kayaked off 25 foot and a 20 foot waterfall. Three of us went off the 20 foot waterfall, and only two of us went off the 25 foot waterfall. I went off both, on "The South Fork of the Rio Grande River", (Colorado Rivers and Creeks book) and that was near Durango. I also helped one of the friends who after bump-sliding over a rock flipped upside down underneath a seven foot waterfall, getting him out while another friend went after his paddle that was downstream and his boat was dented on the nose.

I snow skied at hunter mountain among my fiancé. When I got married, I honeymooned in Grenada, where I jumped off a 17 foot waterfall. I probably should have honeymooned in Florida, although, I enjoyed Grenada. I bought us thatched hats, Grenada chocolate, and we took a cab to a seafood restaurant owned by Grenada twins. I have traveled to Thailand when in 20s (Chiang Mai visiting an economist, Bangkok watching Muay Thai and eating sea bass among ex-wife), Singapore (for 1.5 years among a wife of mine), Myanmar (for a conference on elephant logging), and Krabi, Thailand rented a kayak and paddled that sea kayak among my wife at the time out to an island, and returned among some additional gas boaters, one from the company she for which she worked that took pictures of us.

Two of my siblings, grown to more, have traveled to Egypt and brought back some of the first paper called papyrus or ridden a camel. I read that camels in Australia have "camel milk production, 50,000 gallons a year at last available count...compared with 634 million gallons in cow's milk sales today." (122 Williams National Geographic).

When I was in Singapore, I bought cow milk from Australia at Cold Storage grocery. I also mailed dry milk to Singapore, because, before going to Singapore, I heard one of my wife's co-workers say "there's no milk in Singapore" on the phone when at the New York, NY grocery store a block from mine and my wife's home. That was not true. Maybe she was referring to my ex-wife, and if so, that was rude and not professional, and not her business, and if given more time I would have made milk with my wife, if we weren't asked to fly off to Singapore. I used to enjoy rollerblading near the Hudson among my wife, went on a sushi and sailing cruise, went to watch live music on a water-boat ride to north New Jersey, among taking a sushi making class at a sushi restaurant. Maybe public international companies like extraditing women and their husbands when the woman isn't pregnant but that doesn't seem logical for good people to have to experience. They should have not done so, because my investing missed out because I put stock trading on hold. I did rent a boat to go to Indonesia, and my wife and I would rollerblade near oceanside where the 100 barges I counted on Bloomberg terminal at the library wait near time of picking up cargo. Also, I spent more, and so did my wife on housing, when there is no need for housing in Singapore, since the weather is in the 80s yearly, I wish my wife and I had camped in Singapore—I left my tent, an Osprey backpack, and some of my clothes to her because I was planning to come back to her. We missed enjoying holidays among families including birthdays and Christmas and Thanksgiving. On Thanksgiving my ex-wife had to work so I had ready for her when she arrived home to celebrate Thanksgiving of our hometown country.

When my sibling and my parents came to visit, we went among my wife to the Quays to eat dinner near the water, to vista restaurants overlooking the ocean, on hikes, to Mt. Faber, rented a boat to Pulau Ubin where I spotted a Komodo dragon, rented bicycles there to enjoy, went to Malaysia although my wife missed because she had to work forfeiting the rock climbing at Batu Caves where we climbing using rope as safety catch about a 60 foot climbing cliff on multiple ascents.

I also went kayaking among my brother-in-law at a river in Arkansas soon fairly soon after he was married to her.

I traveled to Key West among my siblings and parents. We stayed at a low-rise hotel, had a good dinner, and awoke to go fishing in rented boats. We caught fish. On the way back to the hotel I saw a guy and his adult son, and the guy resembled someone that I had seen previously. I acted negative towards the man that was walking towards our hotel although he seemed fine afterwards. I wish I had ignored the traveling stranger.

I was in Florida among my siblings and parents, because we were making the best of things, and enjoying each other's company.

Florida being fun, and important to be working for getting food, I want to go back to that hotel on vacation again, camp, and maybe stay some other places, including migrating to and from Florida from TN by foot and maybe boat depending on how easy it is get a boat up a river because I have kayaked upstream previously on the Wolf River in the rain. I want my siblings to go along among also, and to enjoy ourselves even more. We will have to ensure to pay attention to not getting arrested, and probably to ensure camping in places that allow campers along the way, and to ensure access to water.

We had such fun at dinner, walking along the water near shops and a restaurant after another meal. Fishing was great, and I hope to return. I am thinking about going to law school, and if I do then I will probably go either to Memphis, New Orleans, Miami if I can find suitable semi-permanent camping, or somewhere drivable from our family Gulf condo.

I have been to Destin FL many times, and have pictures as a youngster less than teens age, among my siblings. I even have pictures of myself, my siblings, our parents, including some of our friends, including my ex-wife, and some picture of just my siblings and my parents at various ages with catches from charter boats and party boats.

After I came back home, I started fruit tree planting, hiked at Meeman park in the tree shaded hills near the Mississippi River among my parents and my sister who resided in another house in a more densely populated neighborhood than my parents resided. I thought about move to nearer my sister who had a female house-mate, not mate, just a friend, and had gotten a divorce, but I was shy of living in close quarters to many people even though I was thinking about living in a condo near her home. My oldest brother had bought a condo, I just was a little hesitant to live in a dense city after Singapore. I did go to my sisters' and had some deer at a party she held welcoming me back home because my brother had left deer in a freezer from one of his marriages when he lived at that house prior to my sister. I bought a book called *Preserving Food Without Canning or Freezing*, and since the deer seemed about three years old, incorrectly gave some away, although some was given to friends. I should have quickly replaced the old deer with fresh new. I have been giving something to try and make up for my misdirection. I then started making jerky according to a wild game cookbook my parents had, and I used salt for preservation. I started using honey some also again, after reading about honey use in *Preserving Food Without Canning or Freezing*. Best to eat the food in the freezer and good to make jerky, from Eat Like a Wild Man by Gray or another similar book.

I was a little cautious of living near others than my trustworthy siblings because of getting a concussion from an African, a Singapore Slinger basketball jerk, at a musical disk jockey (DJ) party in Singapore when I was looking the other way he punched me I saw out of the corner of my eye that knocked me out briefly and when I came to, I had black eye, bump on forehead and bumps on the back of my head. I knew the guy played with a basketball for his profession because when I was going to get a vaccine, I took the MRT, public tram transportation, and I talked to two basketball strangers in person when traveling for an appointment.

Nonetheless, I kept up exercising and traveling to Florida for fishing trips, and my sister met another guy so I gave them fish from fishing travels at Meeman park. I dated some other people.

I used to kayak the Wolf River among my parents during the summer after coming back home from being abroad. Each of us even kayaked the Ghost River, which is the upper Wolf River, and spotted some cottonmouth snakes that were aggressive swimmers. I plan to do some more boating.

I hiked among my parents to the Wolf River from my parents' house and I wished my sister(s) were there and also would be good for my brothers to come along on that type of home to river hiking in case the police ever show. That's how I would like to migrate, is among my siblings and our family, although at this point, I have to think creatively how that would work and do more to plan.

A Climate Warming Solution Is To Pace Carbon Emissions

My global warming solution is to slow the pace of carbon emissions through energy conservation because it takes a little more than a thousand years for some of the greenhouse gases to escape the ozone once created, according to my research on the internet and climatecontroljournal.com is a source discussing the time for some emissions.

I have some concerns about survival in colder climates. The reason for this is largely due to, first, structural roofs potentially deteriorating (stone or copper (see durability beneath duration subtopic) are good building products), and secondly how long before we run out of clothing? You see, clothes eventually may lose their durability if not kept out of nature's elements. We would need, for survival, constant replenishment of good clothing to survive in colder climates. But mostly a dry roof for sleeping. Because if kept dry and away from sun I think clothes or covers most likely last longer(est), so even if they fray too much to be worn, and fall off then it seems we could use for covers. I don't think they turn to dust, but I would have to study that further. So, say we grow cotton and raise sheep for clothing and warm comfort, or sleep with live sheep, and each other, then how do we stay warm when walking about unless we are handcrafting (without electricity eventually) clothes from natural materials. Poo probably sluffs off. A thin layer on the skin, which dries, cracks and hardens might actually be good sunscreen if someone moves to a warmer climate.

I apologize to my sister for punching the boyfriend she brought once, because it feels that she had a reasonable climate zone invitation although maybe too far from home to Mexico although he was born somewhere else. I just didn't want her going to another country that I didn't want to reside permanently, and I wasn't invited to go with her by his family. There's no excuse on my behalf, although I would rather make a place for her additionally in Florida somewhat more near home, and I should have wooed her more to ensure she would rather not bring guys to the house other than myself our father and brothers and nearest kin cousins that me and my brothers deem acceptable invitees during holidays. To explain, however, I had been punching a punching bag in the United States and practicing according to my Muay Thai boxing lessons in Singapore because of the Chinese cab experience. When I was in Singapore, I called doctor who completed a crossbite jaw surgery on my crossbite from the Muay Thai gym on the phone, who said that the tooth implant was stronger than regular teeth and yes, I could spar. So I was taking classes to get to level two, and took 40 to 50 classes, and I was supposed to take about 100 to reach level two. I took lessons because a Chinese guy punched me while I was exiting a cab in Singapore, I kicked him so that he couldn't enter the cab that he was trying to get into the back seat among me. When my siblings and parents visited, we walked near the gym and I pointed out where I took lessons. I don't recommend punching people. I saw an ex-boyfriend of one of my sisters, and told him I apologize for punching him and wouldn't do that again if he started dating her again. Punching is acceptable in self defense; also fleeing makes sense to get away from harm.

I am considering relocating to a climate zone that is warmer. Anyone can research various states or countries where the climate is nice. I think The Everglades rarely gets below 40F, except in winter it can get into the 20s so maybe I'll try that location approximately. I might need sugar because supposedly sugar helps keep people warm, according to internet research I completed. The body needs to stay in climate at or above 40 Fahrenheit to stay adequately warm according to my quick internet research on the subject, so I suppose clothes to keep me dry and warm; e.g., bivy may be in order. I might, to the extent the ocean rises, retreat to higher ground and I bought a book on the Cumberland Plateau to look at trails in case that is safer higher elevation. Although, my parents' home maybe a good place to be located in the summer.

Caffeine is one thing in warm climates (coffee, tea, cacao ($1/7^{th}$ of caffeine of coffee according to internet)) to be weary of because it causes your 'fight or flight' response to increase, and fighting usually is not a good solution because it can run people off or worst and scary if you get put into jail for fighting. So, moderation is best. Plus, caffeine reduces b-vitamin absorption, which is bad, we don't want to lose those b vitamins ordinarily, maybe good if accidentally taking too much b12. Green tea, although, is supposed to be good for Lyme from internet research I completed, and coffee is remedy to hepatitis, according to the herbal PDR (and hangovers, but please avoid any level of alcohol intake if under 21 and if over 21 more than one cup a day every other day is detrimental according to internet research). My grandparents on one side were t-totalers (meaning they didn't drink any alcohol).

"In Antarctica....part of the food chain" is krill. "Krill are also a carbon sink, eating phytoplankton that have absorbed CO2 and then excreting pellets to the sea floor where it can take thousands of years for the absorbed carbon to resurface (107 Tritram Korten National Geographic). Prince Phillip, ancestor to me according to 23 and me, went to Antarctica, according to the World Book.

Colorado Mountain Hike, Skiing, and Geothermally Naturally Warm Pool

Our church took the youth group on various trips. One of those trips was to Colorado which was about a five or six day hike in the mountains. We split into groups of about seven high schoolers, three guides and three adult volunteers from the church. Hiking in the mountains for that amount of time, we packed our own snacks, and set our own tents, with the guides carrying most of the food. We rotated shovel duty, the team members who dug the dung hole which was covered with dirt before we left, which was probably a good way of fertilizing the trees root, away from the creek. We drank mountain stream water, and used iodine to purify the water. We had a fun time communicating during meals of mostly cheese and Roman noodles for dinner, hiking about 13-15 miles a day, and getting close to summiting a 14,000 foot mountain so we were somewhere in the mid 13,000 foot range where we were yelling back and forth to the guides that we wanted to ascend while the guides said the girl couldn't trek through snow above knee high. So us guys turned around to stay with the group.

On a family vacation, we went to a Rocky Mountain hot springs and went swimming in the naturally warm pool in the snow and had good beefsteaks for a meal. We also went snowmobiling in Jackson Hole, Wyoming, and I saw wolves running in the snow near a creek during the van drive.

Durations of Commodities

After studying commodities, I believe that we have about 300 years left of coal remaining because I computed the residual based on existing reserves and consumption rates that I gathered from the Commodity Research Bureau (CRB) Yearbook, and I get that number through dividing reserves by consumption. Many pesticides come from coal, according to the CRB Yearbook 2008 version. That is one reason I started sales-pitching solar panel because I figure they may help reduce that bad stuff from re-surfacing, since I took ecology in high school I pay attention to finding good things for the environment.

Natural gas, I estimated currently easily findable reserves have about 300 years remaining based on reserves and consumption figures found in the CRB Yearbook. This may extend further out depending on certain factors. I further think that fracking is to find petroleum, and petroleum is used more than natural gas, so there is opportunity to build a natural gas facility to sell heat electricity to the grid to make money, or be energy efficient because the 100 years left of petroleum should be about the same as natural gas for pricing parity, a business school economics term. I found an estimate of reserves in the World Book Encyclopedia. I found it rather peculiar reading about how they use sand to get more petroleum from a reserve, according to *Twilight In The Desert,* of petroleum by pumping sand in to get the petroleum I suppose to where they are able to reach the petroleum. My thinking is that they may need sand in there to prevent sinkholes more than they need petroleum pumped.

Copper, I estimate, will all be in place in about 150 years, using some figures from the CRB Yearbook and extrapolating into the future estimates of growth fueled by more electric cars and construction spending. Some of the figures I protect come from a research report provided via a mining company email distribution, and I met with the chief executive officer (CEO) of that mining company years ago, which is why I get some of the information and data via email. Supply and demand could extend this estimate for copper being in place. It is difficult to know how long insulation materials will last, and I have not found a "degradation" number for copper. Supposedly, a magnesium insulator lasts forever according to its website for copper. And I read online that copper is pure so it doesn't degrade if not corroded or oxidized. A spiderweb is more likely to survive a million years into the future than the internet websites running on electricity, and that's why I own the book *Spiders*, by the Audobon Society. The Bible even mentions that there are spiders in the king's house.

Uranium has a half-life of billions of years, so that could be even better roofing if a roof could be constructed from the ore. Although, it is radioactive; so use underlayment think waterpark design aspects. How badly in ore state the radioactivity is of uranium I am unsure. I read in a Google play book there's about 300 years of easily finable high density uranium raining, and somewhere around 188,000 years of uranium findable in ocean, internet searching.

Go to the internet, where did that go? Well, that's probably going to be the story if copper degrades over time. Electricity may end, maybe I'm wrong, but as of January 2022 I'm employed by ADT solar and there are some things to consider:

First, solar panels degrade across time. If you want to know the exact amount then I suggest buying "Solar Power" by S. S. Mohile and Paul Homes which details that panel output "First year losses = 2.5% LID losses + .7% losses. Second year onward = .7% losses" (48 Mohile).

Petroleum I estimate at 100 years based on reserve figures I found in the World Book and another encyclopedia. Also, consumption figures I got from the CRB Yearbook. We get our tires from synthetic rubber partly that is derived from petroleum according to various internet sources. Depending on the number of times synthetic rubber can be recycled would tell us how long a bicycle tire remains a valid non-obsolete item due to the synthetic rubber aspect of the tire.

Synthetic rubber may become obsolete eventually, with exception of that which is covered by permanent roofing. This depends on its recyclability, for abundancy if roofed. Plastics, I read on the internet a while ago, can be recycled seven times, so my thinking is that synthetic rubber might only be able to t be recycled so many times or eventually I guess it gets left on asphalt or concrete. But we would use less of it if we were all riding bicycles instead of driving cars. So why depend so much on tires? Walking is a good way of life. Walking is probably the best way of life. Exercise improves life, so walk to destinations instead of driving to them when possible.

Therefore, I suggest rationing and reducing your consumption of things such as electricity. Please, folks, hug a tree as I was instructed to keep me disciplined of trouble at grade school age camp for church once.

Building Products

I am a member of the inventors club, thanks to my twin sister adding me on when we were playing in the attic among a neighborhood female acquaintance when we were younger.

I communicated to the Army Corp. of Engineers about bridges doomed to collapse eventually if they aren't made of uranium. Therefore, we need floatable bridges that can turn into ferries if the bridge fails and safety catches for those above, and boat bridges and rappelling cables for bridges to catch the part of the bridges when they eventually collapse, unless the electric grid requires natural gas to overtake uranium spending on electricity, and checks the viability of replacing all bridges with safe uranium bridges with layers to block radiation into nearby goers.

Copper for roofing may be a reasonable solution. Uranium seems best depending on radioactivity and workability because it has tensile strength of steel according to internet research I completed. Also, boat hulls of uranium may be the best invention imaginable.

Copper in Egypt 5,000 years old has been found to be serviceable, according to the CRB yearbook. Oxidation may be something to worry about, and I don't know the duration of copper.

Stainless steel in the elements is supposed to last about 1,000 years, according to an internet resource.

Stacked stone walling makes sense to me. Or mounded dirt or stacking clay, if covered enough to prevent wetness creating mold.

Uranium lighting rods and grounding wires may be best use to reduce money and industrial needs for fire fighting though prevention. Boat hulls and roofing shingles are a want, potentially a need if it keeps jails from being built with uranium. I wonder about holes left for steel ore in the ground about the number of trees above ground before mines were put in place.

The remedy for "radiation" is to use "iodine," according to Dr. William Walsch's book *Nutrient Power* and the quantity of iodine to take is found in Dr. Menell's book The Vitamin Bible as recommended daily amount (RDA) on some product labels that contain iodine such as salt.

Drill Safely to Avoid Making Sinkholes

When drilling for water, oil, and natural gas know the geology so that you aren't digging deep beneath areas that have gypsum or salt, because when those mix with water movement a sinkhole may occur (paraphrasing gypsum and salt from Minerals and Rocks book by National Geographic).

Herbs

Oak is listed in the Herbal PDR as good for "digestion" at one gram of the seed acorn less shell. A Native American Food Plants book shown as herb.umd.umich.edu in Daniel Moerman's book (10), describes "food uses of more than 1500 plants" by Native Americans, and details food preparation while listing the plants alphabetically, mentioning oak. Both books show a picture of what the oak three looks like. Many of the Native Americans are identified geographically and some are named as to what reiver they survive nearest. When you are buying toilet paper, read the oak section before you buy toilet paper that isn't going to be eaten or used by people in jail fighting property that takes lands from people.

The American Pond Lily grows widely at a slew near Memphis where I hope to out-forage the ducks, after I bought some pond lilies at a garden store in Memphis. American pond lily is remedial against gonorrhea, according to my research including The Herbal PDR. Just for the record, I have never tested positive for gonorrhea.

Herbs help to reduce free radicals, according to Dr. Amen's book *The End of Mental Illness.*

Natural remedies for sleep include "melatonin... doses as low as .3 milligram... usually recommend 1 to 3 milligrams...for at least 30 days," ".300 milligrams calcium and 300 milligrams magnesium about 30 to 45 minutes before bed," "L-theanine is a nonprotein amino acid that occurs naturally in the tea plant (Camellia sinesis)..." "Take 100 to 200 milligrams two to three times a day for tension and anxiety and to promote better sleep." (65 Tieraona Low Dog M.D. "Healing Remedies" National Geographic).

Peppermint "tea, for easing nausea, vomiting, diarrhea" "A number of herbs are beneficial for diarrhea: peppermint, catmint (catnip), and ginger" (73) "But my hands-down go-to herb in these cases is Chamomile...quiets intestinal inflammation."

"Echinacea tincture": (99) "Echinacea....for the treatment of fever, infections, venomous bites" o 50 grams Echinacea purpurea herb or E. anguisitofolia root o 250 milliliters solvent, 40 to 60 percent alcohol." I doubt echinacea needs any alcohol. I take Echinacea as a dried herb.

Therefore, this may be better: Echinacea Glycerite, o 50 grams echinacea herb or root, o 280 milliliters vegetable glycerin, o 120 milliliters water

"Licorice relief tincture" (101) "Licorice roots... can be highly effective for inactivating the herpes virus when applied topically during an outbreak." O 25 grams licorice root, cut o 125 milliliters vodka (80 proof)(Nat'l Geographic)

"Insect bites" Witch Hazel tincture (102) o 50 grams Witch Hazel tincture, o 250 milliliters solvent, 20 percent" "apply with a cotton ball several times throughout the day."

Thyme Honey: O ½ cup fresh or 1/4th cup dried thyme, o eight ounces raw honey -if you have a young child in the house (under 12 months of age) substitute maple syrup for the honey in the recipe "for coughs and colds...." "one tspn."

I bought chives at the hardware store's garden center where I was employed, at Lowes. I planted those at my house property near a pond before the creek is in sight. I'm thinking about subdividing out the house or renting it, and then also add in part of the lot to add creek access.

I want to make a can out of the tree that fell, or cut out cups and buckets of wood, canoe, kayak, wooden umbrella, bowls, cups, plates, trays, and I need to buy saws and us saws to craft the wood, unless I should just be there to grow lichens.

I eat some leaves, chew them up and if tastes like to much tannins then I spit some of the liquid out so they are palatable, but not too hard, I spit that too, because want digestible. Sometimes I cook leaves in a frying pan with some water to make tea, and to make the leaves crispier, then I drink and eat.

Good book is Native American Food Plants by Daniel Moerman that describes edibility of Oak, Black Walnut, chives, Wright's Beebrush, Wright's saltbrush, and Tiger Lily.

Indian tribes are identified by geography and practice of food preparation of indigenous plants.

For example, the White Oak "Quereus Alba" is used accordingly, "Iroqious Unspecified Acorns used for food" "The Iroquos live throughout upstate New York and in Southern Quebec" (22 Moerman) "Menominee (206)" (Wisconsin)(23 Moerman) Pie & Pudding Acorns boiled, simmered to remove lye, ground sifted and made into pie. Porridge acorns boiled, simmered..." "...and made into mush with bear oil" "Acorns boiled," cooked in soup tock to flavor, and eaten," (206 Moerman) "Meskwaki (23 Moerman) Iowa) Beverage Ground, scorched acorns made into a drink similar to coffee, porridge dried acorns made into mush."

I read about a peppermint compress being helpful to remedy a headache or sinus congestion in Natural Healing National Geographic special edition (25)

Edible Wild Plants of the West mentions juniper, used as pepper substitute, good for seasoning wild game. Used for making gin. Give berries a day Native Americans.

"Native American Food Plants"

Ojibwas are located in the upper Midwest and Southern Ontario...north of Lake Superior and Huron in Ontario..."

"The Force for Good Foundation is funded by NuSkin Company of Provo, Utah," "...support...sending copies of the book to all 1100...or so registered American Indian tribes and Canadian First Nations... groups" (11).

I know some people in the U.S. that work for NuSkin from the church I visited during my growing years and college when at home, and while in Singapore I went to a Dragon festival party hosted by someone that works in Singapore for NuSkin.

Allium choenoprasum var. sibivicum, (wild chives); Anticosti (40) are "On the Ile d'Aticosti in the St. Lawrence River, north of the Gaspe Peninsula, Quebec. (19 Meorman).

Also, Aloysia Wright's Beebrush "Havasupai" found at the "Cataract Canyon, a side branch of...Canyon in Arizona" (22 Moerman) Beverage Leaves boiled into tea. Twigs boiled to make tea. (41 Moerman) "Greenstripe" "Hopi" "...the Hopi reservation in ...Arizona" (22 Moerman) Starvation Food Used numerous times to ward off famines (As Acanthochiton Wrightii" Vegetable cooked as greens. (as Acanthochiton Wrightii)

Artemesia Carruthii, Carruth's sage wort: Apoche White Mountain, Unspecified species used for food (as A. wrightii) "Navajo, Arizona, New Mexico, and Utah" (24 Moerman). Bread and cake seeds ground and made into bread and dumplings. Porridge seeds ground and made into gruel. (as A. Wrightii). Unspecified seeds used for food (as A. wrightii) Unspecified seeds considered among the most important food plants when the Zuni reached this world (A. Wrightii 32:21)" (55 Moerman)

"Acer negundo, Box elder...Sweetener Inner bark boiled until sugar crystallizes out of it." (32 Moerman) "The vessels are rendered waterproof by the application of pitch secured by boiling jack pine cones." (33 Moerman)

Acer Accharum (Sugar maple)(Ojibwa)(33)" "Cherokee, sweetener juice used to make sugar" (33) "The Cherokees are found throughout much of western North Carolina (particularly Graham and Cherokee counties) and in northwestern Georgia. There are also many Cherokees in Oklahoma." (20 Moerman)

I bought a snowflake obsidian necklace from a Navajo salesperson at the start of a hike in Arizona with my credit card.

"Ariplex Wrightii, Wrights' Saltbush Papago" (61 Moerman) "Papago: In the desert region south of the... of Arizona and extending into Mexico" (25 Moerman). Soup mixed with roasted cholla buds and eaten as a vegetable stew. Spice branches used as seasoning in cooking or pit baking. Vegetable branches eaten as greens in summer. Greens used for food. "Pima". "Arizona' (25 Moerman) Vegetable: Leaves boiled, strained, fried in grease, and eaten as greens. Pima, Gila River. Unspecified. Leaves boiled and eaten. (61 Moerman)

Foraging, Trees Herbs, and tree foods

I enjoy eating cedar sprigs occasionally, and I learned in Moerman's book that cedar seeds are a good water provider and safe to eat. I plan to grow more cedar and eat small quantity, not much at a time.

Chestnut is good for blood circulation, according to the Herbal PDR. I have chestnuts from a tree at my home, and I plan to further cultivate the tree to where there is abundance that I may share and barter or sell some of the chestnuts.

I am growing ginkgo biloba from seed and the correct serving amount is 60mg, according to the Herbal PDR, and I suggest should be taken along with coffee, cocoa, caffeinated tea or something similar.

I eat some tree leaves and enjoy making leaf tea and crunchy leaves using a frying pan, although sometime I just chew and keep the edible part and spit out what I don't want to swallow.

Lichens are growths from trees that lay on the ground. I bought a book on the Medicinal Lichens, and found it to be very interesting, and helped to drive me to eat tree derived foods.

Many white mushrooms seem to be edible and red mushrooms potentially more poisons, so I suggest looking at book *Mushrooms* for more description as to which wild mushroom are good to forage on. If someone inadvertently eats bad mushroom, then they should probably take milk thistle, according to the Herbal PDR.

To Good Health and Happiness

I enjoyed reading every page of The Bible, The Herbal Physician Desk Reference (PDR), and additional herb books. I want to share my knowledge. I enjoyed church among my sibling, parents and that includes Christmas Eve service at a protestant church. We used to go to church every Sunday, and sometimes I work silk ties. A parent to me was an elder in the church, while the other parent taught me Sunday school some years when I was a teenager. Elder sap is used for waterproofing in Native American Food Plants book, while that book suggests the berries are used for food. Keeping attending Bible study and discussion about religion is a way to keep the mind learning, and reading is exercise, latter point according to Dr. Amen. A favorite Bible verse for until, when, and after the sun goes out, is The Bible's Galatians 5:22 "But the fruit of the Spirit is love, joy, peace, longsuffering, gentleness, goodness, faith, Meekness, temperance: against such there is no law." The Golden Rule is civil, "...do unto others as you would have them do unto you." (Matthew 7:12).

Mined minerals such as germanium, which helps provide oxygen when taking anything that would draw from oxygen, is found in onions. I had some germanium taken from me in Sevierville, TN that I kept hidden, and I took a tiny amount of it daily in the quantity that freefitnesstips.co.uk recommended, and it worked fine as I read the entire article. It was just a tiny spec worth of germanium. Be careful not to consume to much of any mineral.

I am thankful for the wonderful memories I have growing up among my siblings and my/ our aforementioned parents. I am also thankful for sustenance, and plan to create a new generation after this to share good experiences among my nieces and nephews.

Wishing good health, in Italian is salud, and happiness for myself, my siblings, my parents, and then for cousins nearest kin before the furthest sequential lineage. Hopefully we can all achieve health and happiness I can only influence and be positively impressionable on those that can hear me, see me, and to learn from me via my writings. So, take adequate levels of magnesium because that is supposed to help prevent depression, get adequate amount of exercise at approximately 30 minutes daily alternating muscle groups every other day from my exercise regime training, and get good sleep one tip for the latter according to sleep.org is to exercise two hours after breakfast or lunch. Also, ensure that you are getting adequate iron, that may be found as yellow in clay, according to the *Rocks and Dirt* book. Good sleep, clean water, correct recommended daily amounts (RDAs) of food and minerals helps. I take a third of a multivitamin daily, and in Singapore I bought Centrum at the grocery. Include antioxidants and even a tiny daily dash of the herb nutmeg because those help eye health and vision, respectively, according to a vision doctor I questioned and the Herbal PDR, respectively, in your meals.

Ensure you are getting adequate vitamin D, that may be gotten in small quantity when mushrooms absorb sun, but as *The Making of the Mind,* that my twin gave to me for our birthday, suggests, get about 20 minutes of sun daily. I would add the amount of time depends on solar irradiance. This sunlight helps to improve happiness when in moderation.

Bibliography

Colorado Rivers and Creeks.
Commodity Research Bureau (CRB) Yearbook 2008.
Druids Book of Medicinal Tree Medicine.
Eat Like A Wild Man. R. Gray
Essential Oils. Dr. Axe
Edible Wild Plants.
Exoplanets.
Herbal Antivirals. Buehner, Steven.
Herbal Physician Desk Reference.
How to Grow Mushrooms.
Medicinal Lichens.
Medicinal Plants of the West. Tilford
Metallurgy. ASM International
Mushrooms. Audubon Society.
Native American Food Plants. Moerman, Daniel.
Niacin, The Real Story. Hoffer, Ahram, M.D., Ph.D., Saul, Andrew, Ph.D., Foster, Harold, Ph.D.
Nutrient Power. Dr. William Walsh.
Rock and Minerals of North America. National Geographic.
Salt. Kurlansky, Mark.
Solar Power. Mohile.
The Bible. King James Version.
The End of Mental Illness. Amen, Daniel.
The Making of the Mind. Kellogg, Ronald.
Twilight In The Desert. Matthew Simmons.
Rocks and Dirt. McHenry, Ellen.
Spiders. Audubon Society.
World Book Encyclopedia. 1984 I think.

cia.gov
climatecontroljournal.com
eartheclipse.com
energy.gov
epa.gov
freefitnesstips.co.uk
sleep.org
sciencetimes.com
worldpopulationreview.com
23andme.com

www.ingramcontent.com/pod-product-compliance
Lightning Source LLC
Chambersburg PA
CBHW041548220426
43665CB00003B/69
* 9 7 9 8 2 1 8 7 6 5 1 6 3 *